BEING **GLOBAL**

BEING **GLOBAL**

How to **Think**, **Act**, and **Lead** in a **Transformed World**

Ángel Cabrera and Gregory Unruh

Harvard Business Review Press

Boston, Massachusetts

Copyright 2012 Thunderbird School of Global Management
Printed in the United States of America
10 9 8 7 6 5 4 3 2 1

Cabrera, Angel, 1967-

   Being global: how to think, act, and lead in a transformed world/Angel Cabrera
and Gregory Unruh.

   p. cm.

   ISBN 978-1-4221-8322-9 (alk. paper)

1. Leadership—Cross-cultural studies. 2. Management—Cross-cultural studies.
3. International business enterprises—Management. 4. International trade.
5. International economic relations. I. Unruh, Gregory. II. Title.

   HD57.7.C32 2012

   658.4'092—dc23

2011046407

The paper used in this publication meets the requirements of the American
National Standard for Permanence of Paper for Publications and Documents in
Libraries and Archives Z39.48-1992.

CONTENTS

BEING **GLOBAL**

Being Global Is Not an Option. It's an Imperative

The headlines today, October 11, 2011, tell a global story. U.S. textile makers are fighting the passage of a free trade agreement between the United States and South Korea because the American manufacturers say Korean technology will put them out of business. Russia has announced its intention to limit grain exports, causing world wheat prices to surge. In Australia, a cap-and-trade bill aimed at putting a price on carbon emissions has just jumped a major hurdle in that country's parliament, sending reverberations throughout the developed world. And Greece, of course, remains a persistent headline winner, as Europe's nations again try to work out a plan so that Greece keeps paying and the euro will remain solvent.

Introduction

The global connections these news stories highlight are not, in and of themselves, new. Global trade has been around, after all, since the sixteenth century (and broad cross-border trade for thousands of years before that). Yet, look to the details and it is clear how much more connected, interdependent, and multidirectional our global world is today than at any time in the past.

Twenty years ago, discussion of a free trade agreement between the United States and a middle-income partner was dominated by debate over which U.S. technologies or industries would most benefit. Today, U.S. manufacturers fear the risk that South Korean technology will pose to the U.S. equivalent. Twenty years ago, it would have taken months or longer for the policy of an agricultural exporter to affect prices at the supermarket. Today, there is a direct line between Russia's announcement and the price of a baguette in Toulouse or, more poignantly, the price the UN World Food Programme pays for supplies to feed drought-affected Somalis. Twenty years ago, the global discussion about energy pretty much started and finished with supply and price. Today, a national energy policy decision by a remote country without significant petroleum reserves affects discussions taking place tens of thousands of miles away. Twenty years ago, the insolvency of a relatively small European country would have made little difference beyond that country's borders and those of its immediate neighbors. Today, it is putting a major world currency, and with it the entire world economy, at risk.

The world economy of today barely resembles that of twenty years ago. A handful of wealthy countries mostly trading with each other or importing raw commodities from poorer ones no longer dominate global trade. Global growth is not solely determined by the innovations or industriousness of developed nations, just like global health cannot be affected solely by the actions of a few. The world today is truly global: inclusive, multidirectional, interlinked, and hugely complex.

In a New Global World, Leaders Need to *Be* Global

The abstract way in which the global actors in the news stories mentioned above are grouped together as "the textile industry," "Russia," and "Australia's parliament" clouds the fact that there are individual people behind those actions and decisions. Those people—people like you, whether you are at the beginning of your career or have witnessed firsthand the impact of rapid globalization, or whether you are bringing your skills to bear in business, in government, or in the social sector—are mostly struggling to tackle the new global environment in all its complexity.

To make matters worse, most undergraduate institutions, employers, business schools, and executive education programs are not yet offering much to help you prepare. It's not that they aren't trying, but despite all the "flat world" rhetoric for most institutions, especially those based in wealthy Western countries, global issues are an afterthought, a set of considerations tacked on at the end of a planning session, not a integral part of what they do and how they do it. Most organizations don't yet realize that global engagement today is not a one-way, hegemonic practice in which all major decisions, innovations, and inputs come from a Western home office. The multidirectional, multifaceted value that can come by tapping into resources, ideas, and innovations from multiple locations is lost on many businesses and individuals preparing for overseas engagements. Just as Western political figures believe that a personal background in business equips them to negotiate multilateral trade deals, so do most businesses believe that they only need to tap a rising star from the home office to capitalize on an overseas opportunity. Give managers some language training and a course in local etiquette and call them prepared.

These *old global* practices are not just insufficient for today's world, they are actively causing harm. Increasingly, they are leading businesses down the wrong path. Walmart's early effort to bring the big-box model to Brazil, where mom-and-pop convenience stores dominate, offers a case in point for how old global practices fail in a *new global* context. Walmart has deep enough pockets to learn from an expensive failure and try again, but not every company has the same luxury.

Aligning the needs, opportunities, and challenges of global engagement requires leaders at the helm who can craft solutions by seamlessly bringing together people and resources across national, cultural, and organizational lines. The skill set of the professionals tasked with overseas efforts cannot begin and end with their reputation at home. They need not only talk but listen; they need not only act but suspend judgment; they need not only bring existing value into a new context but identify where that context can return value and even influence the way headquarters does business. Most importantly, they need to ensure that all members of the relationship benefit. They can't just act global. They have to *be* global.

Being Global: Our Journeys

Both of us have worked in businesses that were drawn into the global market. We, too, have been woefully unprepared—at different times in our lives—to tackle the global challenges we faced. Fifteen years ago, it wasn't clear how an organization that was successful on a local scale could parlay its capabilities to the world marketplace.

That same lack of direction was also common in the universities we attended and where we later taught. It was not that these institutions did not know that the nature of global engagement was changing. They just didn't know how to prepare students to be global. Professors and students alike had difficulty escaping the cultural norms, limited mindsets, local practices, and conservative nature of the academic institutions where we worked. There were efforts to recruit international students, but those efforts were not enough to help those students increase their cultural understanding of the local context or help local students benefit from the increasing diversity on a campus dominated by faculty and staff with little to offer in the form of a global mindset.

In our individual ways, we have each spent the past two decades struggling to learn to be global. Neither of us had a particular advantage in this effort. We did not grow up in multilingual or multicultural environments. Our parents did not move us around the world as children. We had to start on our own. As adults, we have both spent significant time in countries that are not our native homes, acquiring language skills and developing a deeper understanding of the practices and rhythms natural to those countries. We have worked to develop deep relationships with people around the world, people whose experiences and opinions are different from ours. We have looked to identify new sources of value in our work and find ways to share it.

Easy is not a word either of us would use to describe this path, but we are traveling it because we are convinced we must. We believe it makes us better at the things we care about and allows us to better help the people who reach out to us. Greg's deep commitment to environmental issues drives him to continue to learn, cultivate relationships, and attempt to influence the way companies choose their materials, manufacture their products, source their energy, and fulfill their social responsibilities to the communities in which they operate. Ángel's dedication to improving management education, and particularly to promoting ethics and integrity in leadership, drives him to seek connections with academic and business leaders all over the world. Integrity, in his mind, does not stop at the border and in fact is only fully tested when dealing with communities that are distant and different.

Being Global at Thunderbird

Our parallel journeys brought both of us to the Thunderbird School of Global Management, our home institution. Thunderbird was founded in 1946 as an independent, nonprofit graduate school with a mission to train managers for the opportunities in international trade that were expected to grow in the postwar period. The school was located in Thunderbird Airfield No. 1, a decommissioned air base where pilots from the United States and allied countries had trained during World War II. The school's founders saw how people from different cultures had connected. Even in a time of war, people with very different backgrounds, beliefs, and languages could transcend differences. Looking forward, they believed international bridges through trade and investment could contribute to a more prosperous and secure world.

In the more than sixty-five years since its inception, more than forty thousand students have graduated from Thunderbird, and tens of thousands have attended its various executive education programs. Thunderbird alumni include successful international executives and CEOs, government officials, diplomats, development professionals, social innovators, and entrepreneurs. The school's faculty likewise includes world-regarded experts in global entrepreneurship, global management, global finance, global marketing, and international relations, among others. Its single focus on global management has earned it numerous awards, including a number-one ranking among international business school programs, by both the *Financial Times* and *U.S. News and World Report*. The Thunderbird approach to educating the next generation of global leaders is not perfect, but it is the best and most deeply focused we've seen for preparing leaders to thrive in a globalized world.

For both of us, arriving at Thunderbird felt like a kind of homecoming. We had each worked at other institutions, which all lacked the specific global focus we believe is so critical. Being global really needs to be part of an organization's DNA. We both feel that Thunderbird has a unique focus and dedication in educating and preparing students to be global.

The scholarship of our peer faculty members as well as the experiences of our diverse alumni provided us with a rich pool of evidence, examples, and cases to draw from as we were writing this book. Not every leader mentioned is affiliated with the school, but quite a few are. We are grateful for our association with them and the lessons they have taught us. In many ways, this book is not the product solely of our two minds, but of all the minds that teach, attend, and contribute to the institution's mission.

Thunderbird serves not only as a source for this book, but as an inspiration as well. Our students get the benefit of Thunderbird scholarship through the intensive curriculum. But not everyone who aspires to be global can schedule two years in Arizona. Our aim, therefore, is to share Thunderbird's knowledge and experience more broadly. In a way, we've set out to write the book that we wish had been available when we took our first steps toward being global.

Becoming a Global Leader

We have written this book for leaders and aspiring leaders who aim to think, act, and, especially, *be* global and want some help getting there. You may be just starting in a career and creating a long-term plan; you may be in the middle of your career and considering an overseas position or a way to take a different direction.

Our focus on the global aspects of leadership of course relies on a great deal of previous leadership thinking that continues today. We have been influenced by thinkers such as McGill University's Henry Mintzberg; the University of Southern California's Warren Bennis; Wharton's Robert House; University of Washington's Bruce Avolio; Harvard's Rosabeth Moss Kanter, John Kotter, and Nitin Nohria; and INSEAD's Manfred Kets de Vries, to name a few.[1] Their work offers valuable insight, each in their way, for leaders managing people and tackling crises, leaders navigating through change, leaders pursing innovation, and so on.

Where *Being Global* differs from other leadership tools is in its international focus. While the globalization of the world economy has been extensively documented, leadership scholars are yet to fully address the ways in which leadership changes in a global context. Most take the position—either directly or by default—that leading a global firm is not very different from leading a local or regional one: there are the same challenges of securing resources, building and motivating teams, creating and applying new business models, understanding and serving markets, raising and managing capital, and so on.

Our view, however, is that everything becomes much more complex when executed in a cross-national, cross-cultural context. It is not as simple as adopting the proper meal etiquette or learning the language (and anyone who has tried knows even those things aren't so simple). This book is all about the context, the complexity, the connections, and the integrity required when working with different people and cultures.

Other management scholars have focused on how cultural differences may determine the effectiveness of a particular leadership style. This scholarship tradition is rooted in the works of Geert Hofstede and Fons Trompenaars, which has resulted in abundant research on cross-cultural leadership (including the GLOBE project led by our own colleague Mansour Javidan and involving researchers around the world, which we'll discuss in detail in chapter 2). Our focus, however, is not how you can move from one cultural context to another or on how to adapt your style to remain effective in an international assignment. Our interest is in how you can actually *transcend* culture, become effective across cultural settings, effectively interact with culturally diverse individuals and organizations, and create value.

More importantly, *Being Global* is different due to its inward focus. Most existing literature focuses on the outward issues of what leaders do—the actions they take, the words they use, and so on. We agree that the ultimate purpose of self-development is to prepare you to take appropriate action, and in the book, we often show the leaders we profile in action. Nonetheless, our main purpose is to invite you to pause and look within yourself. We are interested less at this stage in what you want to do than in what you want to be and how we can help you become a truly global leader.

Our Global Examples

Each of the people we write about in this book is a global leader; by definition, he or she possesses all the characteristics we identify in chapter 1 as necessary to qualify as a global leader.[2] In most cases, however, we discuss each leader in a specific context in which he or she displayed one characteristic in a particularly inspiring or instructive way. This is simply a function of convenience, not a reflection of the balance of leadership capabilities that person possesses.

It is important to recognize, however, that every global leader—regardless of age or experience or skill level—is always engaged at some level in ongoing self-development. Global leadership skills take a long time to develop, and the path is not straight. On the contrary, it can double on itself, forcing the leader to relearn old lessons for a new situation. The global leaders we profile showed impressive skill at a particular time in a particular context, but that does not mean they are infallible. Being global is kind of like being a black belt in karate: earning the belt requires a great deal of focus, discipline, and ongoing practice, and *keeping* the belt requires the same. Many martial arts disciplines treat the black belt as a starting point or foundation upon which you build for the rest of your life. Any decrease in commitment, a switch to tennis, or even a new sparring partner can all knock you back down.

There are, of course, benefits to falling. It may be tough on the ego, but the different view can reveal where you are and where you still need to go. Consider this book a hand—we'll help you up and show you the way to go. How you continue, of course, is up to you.

We start you on the path in chapter 1 with an overview of global leadership—what it is, why it is so necessary, and what characteristics global leaders possess. We then follow with three chapters that delve in detail into the three core characteristics of global leaders. In the conclusion, we highlight the ongoing work you can do to develop your global leadership skills. The key to this book, and to everything in it, is a deep belief that while you may not have been born a global leader, you can become one. It is up to you.

CHAPTER 1

Global Leaders Can Be Made: Learning to Connect, Create, and Contribute

In 2007, Israeli-born Shai Agassi abandoned his position as the heir apparent of the global software giant SAP AG. He left to pursue a vision of environmentally friendly electric vehicles—an entire world of cars and charging stations, as well as the supply and regulatory infrastructure needed for an electric car to flourish in a gasoline-dominated automotive market. If successful, Agassi's approach would offer a transportation alternative that does not drain the earth's limited supply of fossil fuels or stuff the atmosphere full of greenhouse gases. He also plans to make a lot of money for investors and create thousands of jobs.

Agassi is not an inventor or a government official. He doesn't have any distinct expertise in mechanical engineering or manufacturing, and he doesn't have the power to change transportation regulations or energy policy. What Agassi does have is a set of skills in much shorter supply than any of these resources or assets. Like the rest of the individuals we introduce throughout this book, Agassi is a *global leader*.

What Is a Global Leader?

Global leaders craft solutions by bringing together people and resources across national, cultural, even organizational boundaries. Global leaders are visionaries inspired by a worldwide challenge that remains unsolved, an ignored social injustice or a business opportunity that has gone unexploited. They can identify and call on different individuals who together possess all the pieces necessary to make the vision a reality. These people may speak different languages and be motivated by diverse goals or driven by different values. They may be unlikely collaborators. Global leaders understand the cultural, social, or political differences that keep contributors apart and find ways to build, cultivate, and connect them despite, and sometimes because of, those differences.

In Agassi's case, it was clear almost from the outset that his vision of sustainable transportation would not be possible without the engagement of individuals and organizations spanning the globe, from the public, private, and civil sectors. So Agassi raised venture capital from investors in California, New York, Copenhagen, and Tel Aviv for his firm, Better Place; he reached agreements with the governments of Israel, Denmark, Australia, Hawaii, and California; and he partnered with the Franco-Japanese automobile conglomerate Renault-Nissan.

Agassi is an exceptional human being, but he is not unique. Over the years, we have met many people who share the same ability to form a vision and bring together resources and individuals from around the globe to realize that vision in a way that brings value to everyone involved.

Other global leaders we introduce in this book include Rangina Hamidi, an Afghan woman who launched a textile business in Kandahar in 2002 after the fall of the Taliban; Lalit Ahuja, who help establish Target in India; Merle Hinrichs, founder of the global trade matchmaking firm Global Sources; Bill Browder, founder of Hermitage Capital Management; and dozens of others.

Each of these leaders exhibits the traits and characteristics needed to effectively craft global solutions. They act as bridge builders, connectors of global resources and talent, dedicated to finding new ways to create value. None of them was born a global leader, but they each found a way to become one. They have experienced the difficulties of crossing lines in a world that is becoming more tightly connected yet no flatter, where the nuances and differences across cultures are becoming, if anything, more visible and critical.[1] They have found ways to navigate uneven terrain, close gaps, and make a difference for people around the world. The old adage "think global, act local" does not begin to describe any of them. Agassi, Hamidi, Browder, Ahuja, and Hinrichs *are*— or more accurately, they strive to *be*—global.

Why Do We Need Global Leaders?

The most promising opportunities and the biggest challenges we face today are inexorably global in nature. Our economy, environment, resources, education, and health systems all connect to, rely on, and affect the economies, environments, resources, and health systems in other countries.

Take a mundane example: there are few items more iconic "American" than a pair of blue jeans. Look closer, however, and a decidedly global picture emerges. The cotton may be picked from Peruvian or Ugandan fields, shipped to China for finishing, and then sent to Malaysia to be spun into yarn. The yarn goes to Thailand where the fabric is woven, then to Singapore to be cut, before it is sent to Indonesia for sewing. Labels come from India. Zippers from Hong Kong. Thread from Malaysia and buttons and rivets from Taiwan.

Blue jeans are pretty low-tech as far as manufactured items go. The range of countries and systems involved in their production nonetheless signals a widely acknowledged fact that business in most industries—apparel, automotive, electronics, processed food, and pharmaceuticals, to name a few—has become relentlessly international. The words "Made in _____" on many product labels simply refer to the last stop on a global journey.[2]

International trade is not new, of course. Humans have traded and bartered since they became human. The Carthaginians and northern Africans exchanged goods as early as 430 BC.[3] Wealthy citizens of the Roman Empire were fond of Chinese silk even before they were aware of China. Yet global trade today is different, largely because it is so pervasive and efficient. Virtually every modern sector and every geographic location has the potential to link to a global market.

Plenty of events and innovations had to happen through the course of history to create the ease and speed of transport and communication necessary for these linkages to occur.[4] Today's firms are taking advantage of the enabling environment by investing more heavily in foreign markets, regardless of what, to them, is foreign. Between 1988 and 1997, there were 366 cross-border mergers or acquisitions valued at $1 billion or more; in the following decade, the number of deals more than quadrupled to 1,583.[5] Even during a crisis year like 2009, the foreign direct investments made by companies around the world were twice what they were in 1997 and six times what they were in 1989.[6]

World employment figures tell a similar story: in 1990, multinational corporations employed about 25 million people in foreign subsidiaries—employees working in one country for a company headquartered in another. By 2007, the number exceeded 81 million people.[7]

As global business connections are increasing in their number and value, the nature of international business is also becoming more inclusive, multidirectional, and interlinked. The approach to global business first modeled in the seventeenth century by the Dutch East India Company (VOC) as a hegemonic enterprise, wholly driven from an American or European headquarters, with Westerners dominating the management positions, is gradually disappearing. Global business in the modern era is truly transnational. Innovations, supply chains, talent, know-how, and capital no longer flow west to east and north to south, while commodities move along opposite currents. Instead, players at all locations along the supply chain are influencing and adding value to the products and services that reach the customer. One of the most compelling details from United Nations data shows that in 2010, nearly half of foreign direct investment came from developing economies and half went to developing countries—a major change since 1989, when developed economies received 84 percent of foreign investment, most of which came from their wealthy peers.[8]

Today, the world's largest steel company has its origins in India. Another Indian company owns the iconic British auto nameplate Jaguar. The largest building-materials supplier is Mexican. The most sophisticated semiconductor fabrication plants are in Taiwan. The hub of solar energy technology development is in China. Brazil's Embraer is the envy of Boeing and Airbus.

There is plenty of disagreement over the dynamics, modes, benefits, and costs of globalization. Thinkers with wide-ranging views such as *New York Times* columnist Thomas Friedman, urban studies theorist Richard Florida, historian Robert Kagan, and economists Jagdish Bhagwati, Joseph Stiglitz, and Pankaj Ghemawat have all taken varying positions on the trends, results, and effects of globalization.[9] For our purposes, it does not matter which of these thinkers is eventually proven more right than the others. Our interest is not precise measurements of the state or pace of globalization in the present or near future.

Our interest is to help inspire and develop a new generation of leaders who can make globalization better and fairer for all, or who can, in the language of the United Nations Global Compact, create a more sustainable and inclusive global economy. Globalization is the reality that we live in, and we need global leaders who can thrive in this complexity while leveraging its fundamental forces to have a positive impact.

A global world founded on a global marketplace is a hard-won gift given to us by our predecessors. We have the opportunity to create shared prosperity at an unprecedented level. We cannot take this opportunity for granted—it is not predestined or preordained. It can be squandered and lost. Seizing the opportunity depends on this generation of existing and emerging leaders.

Global Leadership Opportunities, Global Leadership Challenges

Globalization benefits have been distributed unevenly. International commerce has consequences that are not always positive—many people have been excluded from global trade networks, and the very act of trade puts a burden on limited natural resources and the climate. Despite unprecedented growth in world economic output and advances in medicine and technology, there are still billions of people who do not have access to clean water, quality healthcare, a good education, or the opportunity to participate in the institutions that will dramatically affect their lives and futures. These problems can be surmounted, we fervently believe, by global leaders of the type documented in this book. But we need more of them if we are not to let our global inheritance to slip away.

Economists since David Ricardo (who first articulated the theory of comparative advantage in 1817) have documented how market connections can bring enormous benefits, often in the form of economic growth and technological innovation. International trade can bring about advances in personal productivity, health, the efficient use of energy and resources, and food production, just to name a few, by allocating work to places where it can be carried out comparatively better, faster, or cheaper. International investments can help expand markets for existing products, optimize the use of existing capital, and transfer innovations and technologies to locations where they can be best leveraged.

Economic expansion and integration also bring challenges, however. Many of those challenges are more extreme today than any we've faced in the past, expressly because we are much more interconnected than we've ever been (even more than during the often-cited nineteenth-century wave of British-led globalization). The global financial crisis that began in 2007 offers a case in point for how seemingly local issues like increased personal savings in China and rising U.S. home values, low interest rates, and a large third-party market for securitized loan packages could lead to a gargantuan speculative bubble that, upon bursting, could reverberate around the world to affect economies as distant as Iceland and Belgium. In 2011, we are confronting a possible double-dip global recession and a repeat of the global credit freeze, as European leaders fail to contain the contagion of a crisis that started with the public finances of tiny Greece and that has put the very euro on the brink.

Our natural environment is another global system taxed by increased connectivity and growth. We have put severe pressure on our supplies of resources and energy, resulting in dangerous levels of greenhouse gas emissions that are altering established climate patterns. To sate our hunger for more, and more affordable, fuel, we have assumed massive risks, made visible in the *Deepwater Horizon* oil rig catastrophe in the Gulf of Mexico and the escape of radioactivity from the Fukushima nuclear reactor following the Japanese earthquake and tsunami of early 2011.

Global pressures extend beyond energy. Increases in disposable income push demand for animal protein, in turn driving demand for grains, commodities, and water. Mass urbanization stresses the supply of fresh water, energy, and open space. HIV/AIDS, bird flu, swine flu, and other infectious diseases can now spread at the speed of commercial aviation, turning local epidemics into regional or even global pandemics. Poverty and hunger, security, universal education, affordable public health care, equality, and human rights are at once global and local. They are also inter-linked, multifaceted, and hugely complex.

The world needs leaders to capture global opportunities and solve global problems—sometimes with the same vision. We need global leaders to engage with businesses, governments, and nongovernmental organizations, to bridge the distance between these disparate players, all of which have something to contribute on the path to shared prosperity and sustainability.

Global Leaders for All Sectors and Institutions

Global leaders are not born but made. The enterprises, organizations, and governments making strides to capitalize on opportunities and solve problems on a global scale are not leading themselves; they are led by individuals who have invested in developing the skills they need to function—even thrive—in a globalized world. Being global is a personal journey. It is about how you choose to focus your attention, spend your time, and engage your mind.

The payoff for this investment is great, but it is not necessarily measured in the traditional benefits that businesses have come to promise, and business leaders have come to expect, for their performance. Being global is not about earning the corner office, getting the next raise, or watching the stock price tick higher, though those things may happen. Being global and becoming a global leader are instead about the kind of person you want to be and the kind of world you want to live in. The payoff will come through the connections you make, the gaps you bridge, the opportunities you capture, and the solutions you create and that our world so desperately needs. The payoff will come from actively participating in the building of the world you want, not just wishing for it.

Most people on the global leadership path ask themselves what they want to be at many points in their careers: at the outset, at times of transition, even at the point where they begin to slow down. Eventually, that question narrows down to issues of vocation. Do you want to be a leader in business, innovating new products, employing people, and earning profits for yourself and your firm? Do you want to be a leader in government, representing the people and promoting the policies that will make your country a more prosperous and equitable place to live? Or do you want to be a social leader, directly serving your society and its most vulnerable people?

Answering that question is not as straightforward as it used to be. In today's world of unprecedented global opportunity and unprecedented global challenge, the boundaries of influence among business, government, and nongovernmental organizations are increasingly fluid. The classic separation between business and government, most vehemently articulated by Milton Friedman's famous adage that the social responsibility of business is to increase its profits, appears awfully out of sync with a new reality in which businesses are increasingly under pressure to proactively engage in social and environmental issues at best indirectly influencing their bottom line. Even Harvard management professor Michael Porter, best known for his classic models of competitive strategy, has recently argued that business leaders ought to seek "shared value" that would benefit not only their shareholders but society at large.[10] The costs of business are absorbed, after all, not just by shareholders but by the broader society. Consumers increasingly expect that the businesses they support act responsibly toward their employees, the environment, and so on. Businesses likewise find that access to capital and talent depends on the success and health of the societies and economies in which they operate.

Companies do not operate in silos. They are embedded in human and environmental systems in interdependent ways.

Governments and nongovernmental organizations are under similar pressures to reach beyond their traditional boundaries. Budgetary constraints and increasing citizen demands have forced governments to seek out partnerships with businesses to deliver public goods more effectively, from education to health care to security. Nongovernmental organizations have learned to rely on profit-making business models and market-making interventions to address complex economic development problems in financially sustainable ways (from providing microloans to self-employed individuals in poverty to commercially distributing clean cook-stoves, mosquito nets, or solar-powered lamps).

Fortunately, cross-sector collaboration among business, government, and the social sector is giving rise to the same wealth of opportunities as cross-border collaboration among businesses located at different points of the globe. In this sense, *being global* is not just about engagement across national boundaries but engagement across the cultural boundaries that typically separate government, private, and social sectors. Within this ecosystem, businesses often hold the key resources and technologies that they can put to use to address social challenges—and earn in the process. Being global is crucial for leaders in business, government, and the social sector both because each is facing similar globalizing forces and because the very abilities required to deal with a diverse, multicultural world can also be helpful in effectively working with one another.

One place where we see these connections today is in pursuit of the Millennium Development Goals (MDGs), a set of eight development priorities set by the United Nations.[11] Progress on the second MDG, whose goal is to educate the world's most vulnerable children, for example, would not be possible without global leaders cooperating across national cultures and across the public, private, and nonprofit sectors. One notable project, the Global Education Initiative, has brought together UNESCO (a multilateral organization), the World Economic Forum (a Swiss private foundation), technology providers such as Intel, Cisco, and Microsoft (U.S.-based multinational corporations), and investment company Abraaj Capital (a private equity group based in Dubai) in the pursuit of technology-based education solutions in Latin America, the Middle East, and North Africa.[12]

Another innovative and indicative effort, which we discuss in chapter 3, required collaboration between Ghana's teachers union and education ministry, an Indian nonprofit that pioneered and tested a successful literacy program, a U.S.-based research organization, and a collection of funders. Annie Duflo, a leader involved in this effort, saw the opportunity, convinced the necessary government agencies, and sought out the financial resources so that the program, known as the Teacher Community Assistant Initiative (TCAI), could launch.

Though there are some notable successes, building bridges that allow effective cooperation across sectors, cultures, and institutions is a difficult and demanding task. The boundaries between these sectors may be blurring in terms of the problems that affect them, but the toolsets available to each are different, and each imposes different demands on the practice of leadership. Nonprofits, for instance, increasingly must become adept at selling innovative products and services that drive their social missions, a phenomenon known as social entrepreneurship. Governments have likewise needed to learn to leverage market dynamics in the service of policy objectives and take advantage of those same market dynamics to outsource the delivery of public services to private actors. Businesses, in turn, are under increased pressure to engage in social and environmental issues related to their core activities.

Across these blurred lines, global leaders bring together disparate parties with uncommon views and skills in pursuit of common goals. These linkages are particularly important, given the ways in which people working in one sector tend to ignore the effects their actions have on the others. Greenhouse gas emissions offer a case in point. When, in 2007, the European Union set the laudable goal of reducing greenhouse gas emissions, it estimated that some reductions would come through increased use of biofuels in cars. In response, the governments of Indonesia and Malaysia permitted developers to clear virgin rainforest to make way for palm plantations that would produce palm oil to sell to the EU as a biofuel. The conversion of rainforests to agricultural land, however, is a major source of greenhouse gases in its own right, nullifying the impact of the EU policy. A local solution exacerbated a global problem.

Global leaders are able to avoid unintended zero-sum courses of action because they are able to see the world's problems in their complexity. Their solutions may address only one aspect of a problem, but they function in a system of parallel, disaggregated efforts that collectively drive toward a more sustainable and inclusive world. For business, many of those solutions will represent significant commercial innovations that employ thousands and earn millions. Others will belong to society or government. Most, however, will require collaborative efforts by all three sectors.

Global Leaders Connect, Create, and Contribute

Global leaders *become* who they are by cultivating particular ways of looking at the world, thinking about problems and opportunities, and acting with integrity to pursue solutions. The individuals who best master these challenges have invested the time and effort to develop three global leadership competencies. Global leaders, in short, have developed a global mindset, global entrepreneurship, and global citizenship. Their global mindset allows them to connect with others across boundaries, their entrepreneurship enables them to create value through those connections, and their citizenship motivates them to seek a positive contribution.

Global Mindset

Leaders who possess a global mindset are able to interpret, analyze, and decode situations from a variety of perspectives to identify the best route to successful collaboration in a multicultural environment. A global mindset arises through the development of three different types of personal capital: *global* psychological capital, global intellectual capital, and global social capital.

Leaders with significant global psychological capital have the cognitive ability to analyze situations from multiple, even competing, points of view. They have a driving interest in learning about other people's perspectives and are capable of suspending their own judgment in order to more subjectively understand a particular situation.

Global intellectual capital develops in leaders who dedicate time and effort to learning about different parts of the world. Leaders with such capital have strong knowledge of economic and political issues around the world, and they can grasp the inherent complexities of international affairs from multiple national perspectives. Global leaders also recognize how these international trends and events have an impact on their industry and are aware of the major risks and potential rewards involved in operating in various regions.

Global social capital accrues to people whose social networks of friends, colleagues, and contacts stretch beyond one nation or region. Those in possession of strong global social capital display an unusual ability to connect emotionally and communicate effectively with individuals from different cultural backgrounds. They have tact and know how to listen and assimilate multiple viewpoints when making decisions.

Global Entrepreneurship

A global mindset is critical for global leaders' success in building bridges across cultural boundaries, but its true benefit comes when they act as global entrepreneurs and leverage that mindset to create value. That value may come in the form of an innovative new product, a new mode of operation, new forms of financing, or solving existing problems. Global entrepreneurs are both social and political innovators, reaching across boundaries of place and sector to forge value-creating partnerships among business, government, and civil society. They are boundary spanners and "bridgers."[13]

Entrepreneurship may take place in new start-ups or within big companies; it might be a social innovation or a hit product. Value, in our definition of entrepreneurship, is not limited to financial returns for investors but includes other forms of individual, organizational, and social benefits.

Global entrepreneurs create value in many ways. They can tap commonalities, or convergence, between markets and cultures. Conversely, they may tap differences, or divergence. More often than not, they do both. They may rely on convergence around certain technologies to gain access to new markets, while leveraging divergence to adapt their supply chain to the available resources of each country.

Global entrepreneurs may also create value by tapping networks that allow solutions to more widely scale across geographies and sectors. Networks can be as literal as the telecommunications or transportation systems that allow ideas and goods to travel long distances. Or they can be as figurative as the business platforms that allow companies in one place to connect with complementary firms in another. Where the networks do not yet exist, a global entrepreneur may create value by building them.

Global Citizenship

Global leaders are not defined just by their mindsets or by the entrepreneurial opportunities they seek out and create, but by how they contribute to the improvement of the context in which they operate. An individual may leverage his global mindset to build a hugely profitable organization that captures divergent value across borders, but if it exploits local people, destroys indigenous resources, or engages in corrupt practices, that individual is not a global leader. Global leaders act as citizens of the world, pursuing challenges and opportunities in a way that brings benefits to everyone involved.

Global citizenship is probably the most difficult leadership characteristic to master because the business environment often encourages leaders to put private gain ahead of personal integrity. Business leaders in particular are under so much pressure to deliver results for shareholders that they often find themselves able to justify all forms of behavior, such as paying bribes to win contracts, cutting corners in employee safety, or loosely interpreting environmental standards.

Global leaders do not play on the edge of the law. They are moved instead by a true desire to make a positive contribution. Some even pursue a social mission as part of their business.

Rangina Hamidi, for instance, describes her textile handcraft company, Kandahar Treasure, as employing "women artisans from the Kandahar area in order to develop an economic base for the province and support the advancement of women throughout Afghanistan." Shai Agassi calls his company Better Place to embody a vision of sustainable personal transportation. Daniel Lubetzky, an entrepreneur who created Kind Healthy Snacks and PeaceWorks Foods, feels so strongly about the social purpose of his ventures that he has registered the phrase "not-only-for-profit." Business for these leaders is not a zero-sum game with winners and losers. Profit is an outcome from contribution and service.

Even companies that do not have an overt social mission still play a part in transmitting a set of values. Sam Palmisano, chairman of the board and former CEO of IBM, describes his company as a "globally integrated enterprise" in which specific types of work gravitate to where they can be done best, in terms of quality, speed, or cost. In order to coordinate this web of processes, IBM, like other multinationals, promotes a set of core values and standards that hold across geographies. It may globally ban a practice that it considers offensive or unacceptable in one location. While it may seek the path of least resistance in order to minimize costs, it raises levels globally when it comes to values. The idea that one's responsibilities transcend geography or political borders is at the heart of global citizenship.[14]

Conclusion

The next three chapters delve deeper into the three global leadership characteristics. Chapter 2 is dedicated to global mindset, chapter 3 to global entrepreneurship, and chapter 4 to global citizenship. Each chapter offers clear definitions of each leadership characteristic and numerous examples of modern leaders displaying the three characteristics in real situations to address real opportunities and solve real problems.

Each chapter closes with a set of questions that allow you to assess where you are on the path to developing these skills, as well as some actions you can take to develop and improve. These actions are less suggestions than imperatives. Your results are only going to be as good as the work you put into training yourself to be global.

Questions to Ask, Steps to Take

Below we offer some questions and actions to consider right now, as you look for inspiration from global leaders around you.

Question: Who do you know who has been involved in bringing together people and resources from several national and cultural boundaries to success-fully address a global business opportunity or social challenge?

Action: If you know them personally, ask them about their experiences. If you don't know them yet, find a way to be introduced through your social network (through your friends, colleagues, family members, alumni groups, and so on). Ask them: What challenges did you face when addressing the challenge? What sur-prises did you encounter? What did you learn? Did you come up with the right solution the first time? How did your ideas change?

_____

Question: Do you know or have access to successful global leaders?

Action: Arrange to interview them about their life journey. Where did they grow up? Where did they go to school? What jobs and career paths did they follow? What was their biggest failure along the way? What did they learn from it?

_____

Question: How is globalization affecting the industry you work in (or the one you are preparing yourself for)? Who are the global champions in your industry?

Action: Draw those champions' supply chains. Ask yourself: Where do the raw materials come from? Where are products designed, manufactured, and sold? What is the split between national and international revenues? What markets are showing the fastest growth?

_____

Question: How is globalization affecting your city or region, or the city where you grew up? Are there visible impacts on the natural or social environment? How has globalization affected employment patterns and the local business landscape? Is your region dealing with new problems or taking advantage of new opportunities that emanate from the globalization of the world economy?

Action: Reflect on how globalization's effects on your city, your region, or your upbringing have influenced your path, directly and indirectly. Reflect on your own upbringing. How has your education, career progression, and family composition equipped you to deal with cultural diversity? Consider the reactions you have when faced with a culturally tinged interaction you do not understand.

CHAPTER 2

Global Mindset: Connecting Across Cultures

U.S. toy giant Mattel is no newcomer to global business. It has worked with low-cost overseas manufacturers for decades. In 2000, it increased its offshore manufacturing initiatives in China and elsewhere to take advantage of cost-saving opportunities that would allow it to survive within the tight margins of the toy market. By keeping manufacturing costs low, Mattel could focus its U.S. resources on marketing and innovation for the core Barbie, Hot Wheels, and Fisher-Price brands.

The rationale and strategy behind these moves was sound, but their execution was nearly deadly. In 2007, Mattel was forced to recall 19 million toys due to contamination with lead-based paint that originated with its Chinese suppliers. Mattel had erroneously assumed that its partner companies had been using materials and methods consistent with the quality needs of the company and U.S. regulations (they were not at that time).[1]

It was bad enough that Mattel had to recall its products, but it further compounded its mistakes by acting in an old global way: it blamed the recall on its manufacturing partners and Chinese regulatory practices, rather than accepting responsibility for its own failures. Mattel upset not only the supplier, but the Chinese government as well, and the firm had to publicly apologize in order to rescue the future of its operations in China.

New Global Business Requires a Global Mindset

Today's leaders need to react fast to opportunities or risks, often before they have developed the knowledge and skills necessary to properly understand or even perceive them. Like the leaders at Mattel, they work to tap into the comparative advantages of different geographies by chopping up and distributing their supply chains around the world. These leaders outsource design functions to Brazil, IT systems to India, manufacturing to China, and sell products to customers in a dozen countries.

It is one thing to map out value-creating strategies on paper. To capture that value in practice is entirely different.

Where successful global firms stand out is usually not in the quality of the underlying analyses, but in the ability of their leaders to bring together people from different cultures and economic realities. To successfully lead a global organization, leaders need to possess a global mindset. Simply put, being global—by leading and acting globally—requires that you first master the ability to *think* globally.

What Is a Global Mindset?

Our colleague Mansour Javidan defines a *global mindset* as the ability to perceive, analyze, and decode behaviors and situations in multiple cultural contexts and to use that insight to build productive relationships with individuals and organizations across cultural boundaries. Individuals with a global mindset can work with and influence people, organizations, and institutions that are different from their own. They are sensitive to differences, they understand how culture shapes behavior, and they are able to suspend premature judgment, build bridges across cultural boundaries, and nurture trust with others. They are not necessarily proficient in all cultures they interact with, but they find ways to transcend culture to build productive relationships.

A global mindset is a core foundation of successful global leadership; it is a must-have. Yet more often than not, companies regard the ability to think globally as an afterthought. Many make the mistake of assuming that the opportunities in the global economy can be seized via "strategic," top-down, headquarters-driven decisions. They assume that decent performance at home qualifies someone for success in a global role.

We would not go so far as to say that these organizations universally fail. Indeed, some executives do manage to develop their global mindset on the job. But organizations ignore the global mindset of their leadership teams at their own risk. Leaders themselves should sidestep their responsibility for developing a global mindset only if they accept that they are giving up huge opportunities for self-development and value creation within their firms. When proven leaders with unproven global mindsets take on important global projects, they are engaging in a risky and potentially quite painful game.

OLPC and Grameenphone: Lessons in Mindset

Take as an example the nonprofit One Laptop per Child (OLPC) initiative. OLPC is the brainchild of computer science guru and MIT Media Lab founder Nicholas Negroponte. Negroponte launched OLPC in 2005 to deliver inexpensive laptops as learning aids to children in the developing world. Negroponte is convinced that his idea of providing inexpensive computing tools for all children will revolutionize education for the poor. He and his colleagues have vigorously marketed his vision, the laptops that have been designed and built by the project, and its underlying Western-based educational paradigm, to the education ministers of the global South. Negroponte says of his vision that it allows communities to "plant trees of the future . . . by enabling children to engage in collaborative, creative, joyful, self-empowered learning."[2] While close to 2 million XO laptops, as they are called, have been distributed as of mid-2011, most of the world has not signed on to Negroponte's project.

Many education ministers in low-income countries have been indifferent to the promises of OLPC. Their school systems already struggle with limited electrical infrastructure, huge deficits of qualified teachers and physical resources, outdated and irrelevant curricula, and major issues with teacher and student absenteeism. Given these challenges, few of them felt that devoting their entire education budgets (which for many countries is what it would cost to achieve the OLPC vision) to laptops was a sound use of funds. Meanwhile, experts in development economics and education have highlighted a number of alternative programs to improve attendance and quality of education at lower cost and with greater relevance to the community.[3]

The OLPC model is grounded in a rigid set of assumptions that don't leave much room for adaptation: the tool must be a laptop, not a refurbished desktop or a smartphone; computers should function as personal instruments, not as shared resources; the governments should buy the machines and distribute them to the children, and so on. Recently, OLPC has been waffling on the laptops in favor of a tablet computer prototype—the XO-3—inspired by the trendy tablets produced by Apple and others, not driven by a specific need or want of those they aim to help.

No matter the merits of the OLPC vision of empowering the poorest children in the world though computer-based education, results will continue to disappoint until the execution is guided by a deeper understanding of the cultural and institutional realities of developing-world education, which varies considerably from country to country and region to region.

Contrast the OLPC approach with that of Grameenphone.

Envisioned by Iqbal Quadir, a Bangladeshi immigrant to the United States, Grameenphone was one of the first attempts to put mobile phones in the hands of the poor. As a child, Quadir experienced firsthand the costs of living in an environment with a poor to nonexistent telecommunications infrastructure. He once walked six hours to a neighboring village to pick up a prescription from a doctor, only to find the doctor had traveled to another town that day.

An investment banker by training, Quadir spent several years forming impressive partnerships with organizations around the globe: American and Japanese investors, the Norwegian telecom company Telenor, Finnish equipment providers, and, of course, Grameen Bank, the pioneering Bangladeshi microfinance institution. At its launch in 1999, the Grameenphone program allowed female clients to take out a loan from Grameen Bank for the purpose of buying a mobile handset and prepurchased minutes. This "village phone lady" then sold the use of the handset by the minute to other villagers. The whole scheme rested on whether the villagers found enough value to pay for use of a mobile phone out of their limited budgets.

Quadir emphasized mobile phones because as voice-based tools, anyone can use them, even people who are illiterate. They also bring immediate economic benefits. Quadir recounts a story, for example, of seeing those economic benefits in action:

> I once ran into a barber in Bangladesh who, after confronting exorbitant upfront cost of renting a street-front store, abandoned the idea of renting space for his barbershop. Instead, he purchased a cell phone and a motorbike. He used the phone to schedule appointments with his clients and rode to their homes. He was able to increase his fees for the convenience of in-home service. Customers also saved time. The barber was able to serve a larger area with a greater customer loyalty. It is through these and countless other examples that economic empowerment takes hold for people in poor countries, who can then make their own choices to increase possibilities for prosperity for future generations.[4]

Today, there are more mobile handsets in the developing world than in developed economies. Demand for mobile phones has crossed geographic and socioeconomic boundaries, rendering Quadir's initial distribution strategy—the village phone lady—quaint. But in 1999, mobile phones were considered an innovation for the wealthy. Quadir's ability to recognize a real need and forge partnerships across multiple cultural boundaries sowed the seeds for what is now a trillion-dollar-a-year (and growing) industry.

After slightly more than a decade, the village phone ladies are largely out of business because all their clients now have mobile phones of their own.

Now contrast these two approaches. The visions in both cases were not all that different. Both initiatives saw value in bringing a technology developed in the rich West to serve a need in developing economies. Yet the OLPC model followed a traditional centralized, top-down, one-way approach, while Grameenphone adopted a distributed and grassroots model based on a deeper understanding of the cultural and institutional peculiarities of the markets being served. In our terminology, Grameenphone and OLPC both had global visions, but Grameenphone was led with a global mindset, and OLPC was not.

Managing Supply Chains and Mergers with Mindset

Mattel's troubles in China or OLPC's around the world may have the excuse of a significant geographic and cultural divide, but relative geographic proximity does not ensure success in the global marketplace. A global mindset is required even between neighbors.

Take Airbus: after the lavish 2005 unveiling of its eight-hundred-passenger, A380 multideck megaliner in Toulouse, France, Airbus experienced a series of delays caused by miscommunication between design teams working in different European countries (wings from Wales, wiring from Germany). The firm did eventually deliver the first operational planes in 2007, but they were two years late and more than $6 billion over budget, and cost the firm even more in stock valuation and credibility with customers. This history continued to plague the A380 into 2010, when the model experienced an inflight accident involving its Rolls-Royce engines.

Airbus's troubles were not caused by failures of engineering or technology, but of leadership. A vision that brought together individuals and organizations from different cultural settings required globally minded leadership, which didn't seem to be available.

On the flip side, consider the case of Yang Yuanqing, chairman and CEO of Chinese computer manufacturer Lenovo. Lenovo became the first Chinese company to acquire an iconic American business brand when it purchased IBM's personal computing business, including the ThinkPad, in 2005. Hailed as a harbinger of things to come, the acquisition put Lenovo under intense scrutiny. It would have been easy for Lenovo to succumb to the pressures of integrating two different companies from different parts of the world. After all, almost half of all mergers and acquisitions fail to meet their revenue and cost-savings targets, even when the two companies come from the same country.[5]

Born, raised, and educated in China, Yang rose through the ranks at Lenovo and became CEO before the IBM transaction. Yang's upbringing and career had not been global by any stretch of the imagination. But what set him apart was his understanding that Lenovo was a global business and that, in order to be successful, he and the rest of the company's leadership needed to think and act globally.

Yang took a number of steps—some symbolic, others more consequential—to signal to the new combined company the importance of a global mindset. For instance, Yang and his family moved to Raleigh, North Carolina, the headquarters of the IBM PC business, so that he could improve his English and expose himself to the American culture he knew he would now need to understand. He also decreed that the company had no headquarters—not in China nor in the United States. He expected senior executives to travel to different key locations. Quarterly and annual meetings of senior executives and board meetings rotated to different world locations.

Of four core company values, one explicitly declares "teamwork across cultures" as the foundation of how the company works.[6]

Global leaders like Yang and Quadir understand the importance of bringing out the best from people regardless of where they sit or what language they speak. They bring together people, resources, and ideas in pursuit of new solutions. In short, they have and strive to develop a global mindset.

Understanding Culture

By definition, a global mindset is the ability to perceive, analyze, and decode behaviors and situations in multiple *cultural* contexts, and to understand the dynamics of the interactions between multiple *cultures*. But what is culture?

When we talk about culture, we are referring to a form of collective memory that encodes patterns of behavior that have proven useful for the survival of a community. Culture is a set of social norms that can become entrenched on any number of levels: familial, tribal, regional, national, and lingual. The way we dress, the food we eat, the songs we sing, the language we speak, the tools we use, the rites we celebrate, the games we play, the way we court, and the stories we tell: all are defined by and define our culture. Culture determines which behaviors are permissible in a particular context and which are not. Cultural expectations make life easier, in a way. They limit our options, so we don't need to consider every aspect of our behavior anew each time we interact with another human being.

Culture differs widely from country to country, even between neighbors or regions that share a common history. Try to eat a meal in a private home in any country that is not your own, and you will confront very quickly the pervasiveness of cultural difference, from where people sit to who is allowed to eat first to the proper etiquette for toasts. Yet the fact that people in almost every country eat certain meals at certain times of the day points to the existence of cultural universals or categories of behavior across cultures. The late anthropologist George Murdock of Yale University documented those universals in his work. Murdock's list includes fifty-nine wide-ranging items such as mealtimes, hospitality norms, hairstyles, food taboos, penal sanctions, and etiquette.

And yet as much as they differ, human cultures are also remarkably similar in some key respects. There are indeed some universal behaviors that are considered acceptable or unacceptable, regardless of where you come from. Harvard Business School professor Paul Lawrence identified a set of universally accepted behaviors in his efforts to create a model for leadership. His universals include telling truths and not falsehoods; sharing information that may be valuable to another person instead of withholding it; respecting others' property; keeping one's promises; and returning favors, among others.[7]

The management scholar Geert Hofstede went one step further to quantify and simplify the dimensions that make one culture different from another in a work context. Hofstede's statistical analyses of thousands of surveys of IBM employees collected around the world identified such cultural dimensions as power distance within a culture (i.e., how do people behave toward those they view as senior to them) and uncertainty avoidance (i.e., how comfortable or uncomfortable people feel in unstructured situations). Managers entering business relationships in new global contexts have relied on Hofstede's insights to guide them, as have many students of international business.

Mansour Javidan and Mary Sully de Luque, two of our Thunderbird colleagues, are expanding this body of work through the Global Leadership and Organizational Behavior Effectiveness (GLOBE) project, the most ambitious research endeavor to date aimed at understanding the interrelationships between societal culture, organizational culture, and organizational leadership.[8] Launched in 1992 by Robert House of the Wharton School and led today by Javidan, GLOBE has combined the efforts of 170 scholars from 61 countries to survey more than 17,000 managers in 62 different societies. Analysis of the resulting data has allowed Javidan and his colleagues to identify cultural differences in leadership, scale those differences, and create a profile of outstanding leadership for each society.

The GLOBE team has defined nine common cultural dimensions affecting leadership style that will work in any given environment. The dimensions include: performance orientation, assertiveness, future orientation, humane orientation, institutional collectivism, in-group collectivism, gender egalitarianism, power distance, and uncertainty avoidance. The GLOBE work rates cultures as "high," "moderate," or "low" on any given dimension (see table 2-1 for the dimensions and questions that define them). The results from the GLOBE project leave little doubt that national culture not only shapes behavioral patterns but determines the leadership style that is most effective for the context.

Assertiveness, for instance, may be an asset for leaders in one culture and a liability in another. Cultural nuances occur inside national borders as well. The performance-oriented culture in the United States generally values assertiveness. That value sometimes translates into stereotyped views of Americans, often exaggerated in Hollywood movies that depict American leaders (coaches, managers) as yelling, aggressive demagogues. Yet, aggressive leaders do not succeed in every American workplace.

TABLE 2-1

GLOBE cultural dimensions

Performance orientation	Are individuals in the culture rewarded for individual performance and excellence?
Assertiveness	Is assertiveness common and valued?
Future orientation	Do individuals plan for the future, delay gratification, and otherwise engage in future-oriented behaviors?
Humane orientation	Are fairness, altruism, generosity, and caring behavior valued and encouraged?
Institutional collectivism	Is collective distribution of resources throughout the broader society encouraged and rewarded?
In-group collectivism	Do individuals express pride, identification, and loyalty with their families and their close associations (such as loyalty to an employer)?
Gender egalitarianism	Do members of this culture work to minimize gender inequality?
Power distance	Is power distributed equally among participants regardless of social, professional, or financial position?
Uncertainty avoidance	Do individuals rely on social norms or rules to alleviate the unpredictability of future events?

Gary Convis, the former chairman of Toyota Motor Manufacturing, Kentucky (TMMK), witnessed this firsthand in the 1980s at NUMMI, the General Motors–Toyota joint venture that was Toyota's first manufacturing effort in the United States. Some of the Japanese leaders who came to the United States to run NUMMI and train American workers tended to launch into lengthy tirades when the workers made mistakes or acted on misunderstandings. The skilled, experienced workers threatened to walk off the job after these outbursts. Only after Convis, the plant general manager at the time, explained privately to his Japanese mentor how the workers preferred to be corrected did the yelling stop. The Japanese managers developed a softer approach—one that allowed the company to retain and develop its American personnel, which ultimately led to Toyota's rise to the top of the global auto industry.[9]

Possessing a global mindset can reduce the chances of missing important cues or even behaving outright offensively. A global mind is as critical for leaders newly entrenched in a non-native culture as it is for those who regularly engage with multiple cultures.

The Three Elements of a Global Mindset

Cross-cultural organizational research of the kind epitomized by the GLOBE project offers insights into what makes us different, but is not sufficient to explain the skills necessary to navigate complex cultural landscapes *in spite of* those differences. In 2004, Javidan and a team of researchers at Thunderbird launched the Global Mindset Initiative to understand the skills, personalities, and attitudes that allow successful global leaders to navigate the challenges of international business with apparent ease. Their research is finding that those individuals share an extensive set of cognitive, emotional, and social characteristics, which they break down into three forms of "global mindset capital": psychological capital, intellectual capital, and social capital.

Psychological Capital

Psychological capital refers to personal attributes such as openness to new experience, cognitive flexibility, respect for and curiosity about other cultures, and willingness to engage and work with people of other cultures. Individuals with a high degree of psychological capital can look at a situation from multiple angles, apply alternative cognitive frameworks to decode a given situation, and suspend their disbelief to understand how facts may be interpreted through various cultural lenses.

As the earlier discussion about culture makes clear, altering or changing your default psychological makeup is challenging work. All human beings, regardless of how smart we are or where we come from, place new knowledge and experience into existing mental frames we've formed over time. Culture shapes to a great extent how we frame or interpret information, and our brains are wired to protect those frames. We have a number of unconscious ways of doing that, one of which is to highlight evidence that supports what we already believe to be true and discount or reinterpret evidence that points in another direction. This bias allows you to get through the day; imagine how long it would take to make the simplest decisions if you had no prior understanding about what is dangerous or safe, or what others may consider appropriate or distasteful. But there is a downside: your existing frames can cause you to misinterpret information from outside your experience, especially when you are trying to find solutions in a cross-cultural context. Global psychological capital provides the ability to suspend judgments and biases, or at least recognize them and the role they play in your actions and decisions.

None of this is easy. Of the three forms of global mindset capital, psychological capital is the hardest one to develop because it is so firmly tied to personality traits that are formed early in life. Openness to experience, for example, is one of the "big five" traits that social psychologists consider part of the core of one's personality that remain stable through adulthood.[10] There are techniques and tools that can help those who are not born with a personality that makes the development of global psychological capital easy.

First, we can measure psychological capital and therefore use it in identifying weak areas or even complementary partners and team members. Second, we can strengthen it through practice. Finally, the other two forms of capital can compensate for weaknesses or gaps in our psychological capital.

Intellectual Capital

Intellectual capital refers to our concrete knowledge and understanding of the environments in which global interactions take place. Intellectual capital gives you insight into the relevant dynamics of local and regional political systems, ethnic, social, or tribal groups that make up a country's populace and how they have historically worked together, the history of interaction with various cultures, the rules of engagement around personal relationships, the competitive dynamics, the operating policies and regulations, the dominant players in various industries, and so on. Global intellectual capital includes the simple accumulation of facts and knowledge, but it also includes the ability to interpret those facts so you can decipher what is happening in a cross-cultural situation.

Because global intellectual capital is built through learning, it is by definition more malleable than psychological capital, which is rooted in stable psychological traits and cognitive styles. But its acquisition nevertheless comes at a price. It requires investments in learning and the accumulation of personal experiences in various environments. Most importantly, it requires learning to learn: you need the ability and predisposition to ask questions repeatedly and not assume you know the answers. You need to observe, study, and cultivate the endless curiosity needed to figure out how places operate.

Social Capital

Social capital refers to the web of relationships you have with people in different cultural settings. As management scholars Janine Nahapiet and Sumantra Ghoshal have defined it, social capital refers to "the sum of the actual and potential resources embedded within, available through, and derived from the network of relationships possessed by an individual or social unit."[11] Social capital thus comprises both the network of our personal contacts and the assets we can mobilize through those contacts.

Despite the ease with which people today can connect through online social networks, social capital isn't simply a measure of the quantity of connections but a measure of the quality, diversity, and structure of those connections. Social capital is built around trusting relationships with individuals who in turn can provide access to valuable relationships and resources. When it comes to a global mindset, the social capital that is required must be global in nature: it must include relationships across national and cultural boundaries.

Global Mindset Capital: Mutually Independent, Mutually Reinforcing

That we call the three dimensions of a global mindset *capital* is not casual. In economics, capital refers to accumulated assets that can be used to produce other goods without exhausting their value (unlike raw materials that are transformed into other goods). Capital stocks are built over time through saving and investment. Just as intellectual capital requires investments in learning and accumulation of information and insight, social capital too requires investments over time in creating and cultivating relationships.

The three components of a global mindset are both complementary and mutually supportive. The capacity to suspend your judgment and accept that there might be alternative ways to interpret reality (psychological capital) can help build trusting relationships (social capital), which can in turn be a source of new insights about a specific environment (intellectual capital). Knowlege of important facts and dynamics in a given market (intellectual capital) can guide efforts to expand your network (social capital) and can make it easier to accept alternative interpretations of a set of circumstances (psychological capital).

Developing a Global Mindset: From Culturally Illiterate to Culturally Agnostic

A global mindset is not an innate trait. Developing one requires ongoing investment in personal development through both formal and informal education, which helps you transition through various stages: cultural illiteracy, awareness, intelligence, and agnosticism.

Most of us start our journey before we have had any exposure to a culture other than the one we grew up in. It is nearly impossible in this state of cultural illiteracy to understand the role culture plays in shaping social conduct. There is only one point of reference. Like the prisoner in Plato's cave, a culturally illiterate person does not possess sufficient perspective to comprehend how different cultures shape human interactions or how so many of the patterns of conduct that appear so familiar are manifestations of deeply programmed cultural routines, which Geert Hofstede so aptly named "software of the mind."[12]

The first time you are exposed to another culture for a meaningful period of time, you begin to lay the groundwork for developing a global mind. Like all beginnings, this one is likely to be a mix of excitement and pain. When you first arrive in a foreign culture, your dominant feeling is likely to be excitement, a kind of honeymoon phase where everything is new and different and wonderful. Pretty soon, the challenge of functioning in this country becomes clear, and you are very likely to slip into culture shock, which is simply a psychological manifestation of your inability to interpret what is happening around you. Culture shock most clearly shows up as a feeling of isolation or loneliness, sometimes frustration (and can recur unexpectedly no matter how practiced and aware you are of other cultures).

As you move through a new culture for the first time, you engage in a process of experimentation and adaptation in order to function effectively. In subtle or explicit ways, you will feel punished for behaviors that feel normal to you and rewarded for unfamiliar ones you gradually uncover. You may find, for example, that the way you like to sit, hold your dining utensils, or hand someone a business card is perceived as rude. This painful learning process will over time allow you to fit in the new environment. It may also make you culturally aware, meaning that you will understand which of your native behaviors you can still retain in this culture and which you must discard.

Though useful, cultural awareness is not synonymous with having a global mindset. It is really only a stage—and a fairly early one—on the path. Cultural awareness comes about through exposure, knowledge, and expertise in a non-native environment. It is the outcome of effective adaptation to a second culture, but it does little to help you with a third. In fact, it would be materially impossible to develop a deep level of experience with every culture you may come in contact with throughout your life. There isn't time, and could be quite misleading if you're then put in a situation where you have to interact with a new culture. If mindset were only about awareness, you'd have to start fresh every time.

Thankfully, after you have had extensive experience in two, and often more, non-native cultures, some patterns may begin to emerge. You may develop a metacognitive understanding of how culture shapes behavior—both your own behavior and that of others. You may develop the ability to reverse-engineer a culture code and reflect on what differentiates one culture from another. This ability has been referred to by some researchers as *cultural intelligence.*

These stages of increased cultural sophistication help you deal with complex cross-cultural situations. They may lead eventually to becoming culturally agnostic, meaning that you can transcend culture by developing metacultural behaviors that will be effective across cultures.

By framing the development of a global mindset in stages, we hope to make another very clear point: the qualities that enable a person to decode and interpret different cultural contexts are not wired but acquired. Innate individual differences may predispose individuals to developing a global mindset with less effort than others, but every individual needs to work to acquire it.

More importantly, perhaps, everyone needs to work to *maintain* it. This path from cultural illiteracy to cultural agnosticism does not really have a terminus. You probably can't slip all the way back to illiteracy through everyday means, but the impulse to regress to earlier stages, or succumb to culture shock, is very strong, even for those who have achieved agnosticism in the past. The problem probably lies with our brains. It requires an enormous amount of cognitive energy to not default to base interpretations led by our natural biases and mental and emotional shortcuts. Maintaining the ability to see through culture to metaculture requires ongoing discipline, awareness, and humility.

The Global Mindset Inventory

As with any set of skills you want to acquire or improve, it helps, when setting out, to know where you are along your growth path. As part of the Global Mindset Initiative, Javidan and colleagues have developed the Global Mindset Inventory (GMI), an eight-minute survey consisting of ninety-one questions designed to measure the specific intellectual, psychological, and social attributes that enable a person to influence individuals, groups, and organizations from different sociocultural systems.[13]

Tested with fifteen hundred managers in different business disciplines, the GMI is primarily intended as a developmental self-assessment tool (a 360-degree version is also available for team-based assessments). Individuals can use it to identify weak areas in their global orientation. Companies can also use the tool to assess whether its leadership development programs are indeed equipping employees with the skills they need.

At Thunderbird, for example, we use the GMI with our students to allow them to assess where they are in their development when they arrive at the school and where they are when they leave. The student can look at the data and see in which areas of global mindset capital he or she needs to invest the most. For the institution, the data allows us to identify ways to refine the curriculum to better meet the aim of preparing the next generation of global business leaders.

Benefiting from a Global Mindset

One of the great benefits of possessing a global mind is that its advantages begin to pay back, even while you are in the process of developing it. Identifying and unlocking entrepreneurial value—the subject of chapter 3—is not the only benefit that those with a global mindset derive. An advantage of possessing a global mind is that it makes you more resilient to the quotidian challenges of living and engaging with other cultures.

Culture shock offers perhaps the most common and visible example of how this resilience operates. Anyone who has lived in a culture foreign to him or her is likely to have experienced the frustration of dealing with culture shock. When Ángel first went to the United States to live in Atlanta as a doctoral student, for example, he used to take long walks to explore his new city. Whenever he went on one of these tours, the police would stop him on the street to ask if he was okay. Sometimes it even happened twice during one walk. He used to get so annoyed and confused that it really took the pleasure out of a simple stroll. Did he look suspicious? Was he bothering anyone? What kind of city didn't encourage people to just walk around?

Of course, this perspective was borne out of a state of culture shock. Anyone who has spent time in Atlanta knows that many parts of the city are not really meant for pedestrians. There are large areas where the only people who walk further than a few blocks do so because they forgot where they parked. Ángel later learned that some of his most frequent destinations were among the most dangerous parts of town. From that view, the police were just doing their job, a point he eventually came to appreciate.

Culture shock can even occur within a given culture. Greg often says it was harder for him as a Californian to adapt to living in Boston than to life in Madrid. The shock came probably from the expectation that life should be similar and predictable anywhere in one's home country. The reality, as most Americans know in theory but forget in practice, is that Californians have a distinct set of cultural norms from northeasterners.

Culture shock can also happen in reverse to people returning to their home country after a long absence. It can be painful to see the culture you once regarded as home through different, less idealistic eyes. Ángel's wife likes to say she had an easier time adapting to life in Spain as a newcomer than he did as a returnee. She could list endless disputes he had with indifferent government officials, unresponsive customer service agents, and managers of smoke-filled, slow-serve restaurants.

For many, reverse culture shock can initiate a period of deep and profound analysis of who you are and where you are from. *Washington Post* journalist Raju Narisetti, a native Indian and one-time editor of the Indian financial newspaper *Mint*, wrote of his return to India:

> After several futile days of looking at apartments, I was shown a very nice flat . . . The landlady was around and we had a pleasant chat about my decision to move back to India for work reasons after almost two decades away . . . In turn, she told me about many of her son's friends returning from the US . . . It was all quite nice and friendly.
>
> When the broker went back to make an offer she told him I "wasn't foreign enough" for them. In many parts of the world that I have lived . . . landlords didn't want to rent to foreigners, say non-Americans, including Indians. And, here I am, back home, only to be told that I am too Indian for comfort.[14]

The culture shock phenomenon shows that adapting to a new culture, even one we've experienced before, is psychologically costly and painful. This is where having a global mindset helps. Having the openness to new experiences and the ability to suspend judgment that comes from global psychological capital allows you to experience what is happening, accept it as an invaluable learning opportunity, and maintain the metaperspective needed to see through culture to the commonality. Having global intellectual capital gives you the knowledge of the culture necessary to interpret and understand a lot about the modes of interaction, the social structure, the business environment, and so on. Global social capital, for its part, perhaps does the most to allay loneliness and provide you with an anchor of human contact, while also helping you develop the other two. Having someone in the country—or at least someone who can connect you with resources in the country—makes it so much easier to fill in the blanks of any missing context, to ask questions and get a deeper understanding of why certain situations unfold as they do, or even to simply practice your language skills.

None of this means that leaders with a global mindset do not experience culture shock. They do. But possessing a global mindset provides, as mentioned, a kind of cognitive resilience to the challenges of living and working in a new environment. Global minds make transitions into new environments more smoothly—and often more quickly—than their peers.

Internationalist Culture: A False Shortcut to a Global Mindset

For aspiring leaders who travel frequently on behalf of their employers, we have a note of warning. The work required to develop global psychological capital, global intellectual capital, and global social capital cannot be conducted, for most, in the "if it's Tuesday this must be Belgium" travel cycles that many companies demand of their high-potential employees. Accumulating stamps in your passport does not inevitably develop your global intellectual capital and does not always help you build social capital or allow you to test your psychological capital. Many executives who travel for work have such full schedules that they have no opportunities to step beyond the international business institutions and facilities that exist to support them. In these places, the culture is not "German" or "Chinese" or "American," but rather "international" or, more accurately, "internationalized."

It's perhaps easiest to see this culture in the business class hotels in virtually every major city. Waking up in the Sheraton Addis Ababa is virtually identical to waking up in the Pan Pacific Vancouver or the Hyatt Regency São Paolo. Travel is certainly an important part of developing a global mindset and psychological capital, but business leaders need to beware of the tendency to travel without actually crossing any cultural boundaries.

Different Histories, Global Mindsets

Now that we've told you what a global mindset *is*, we want to introduce some remarkable examples of global mindset from our experience.

Jon S. von Tetzchner, the cofounder and former CEO of Opera Software, for example, is a global leader who built a global mindset not only for himself, but for the benefit of his firm.

Von Tetzchner grew up in Iceland and was educated and lives in Norway. The business he founded creates Web browsers for use on computers, mobile phones, and game consoles. From the beginning, Opera Software took a counterintuitive approach to growth. Most firms establish themselves in their home markets and then expand overseas, first to geographies with a common language or a large expatriate population. Von Tetzchner instead focused on markets outside Scandinavia, including emerging economies, which often operate with lower bandwidth and poorer telecommunications infrastructure than his home market. "We had to be accepted outside Norway to be accepted in Norway," von Tetzchner has said about his company's chosen path. "People will not choose a piece of software in Norway just because it's Norwegian. If you get to be popular outside, then they are proud of that, and then they will use your software."[15]

When von Tetzchner started the firm in 1994, he tried to build a global mindset into it from the start. To do that, early on he hired a number of employees who were living in Europe but came from different cultural backgrounds. His intention was visionary yet still practical. Given the firm's strategy of targeting emerging markets far away from headquarters, he needed people with the global psychological capital that would enable them to see the linkages or similarities with other cultures, the global intellectual capital that allowed them to understand the business environment in target regions, and even the social capital that could serve them in targeting those geographies. Von Tetzchner's willingness to look outside Scandinavia—and even outside Western Europe—for business associates and markets points to his inherent psychological flexibility as well as his understanding that stocking his firm with global minds would be necessary for Opera to execute its global business strategy. By creating a diverse cultural environment, he was also building a training ground that allowed each of his associates to cultivate his or her own psychological capital.

It would be easy to look at von Tetzchner and conclude that he had an advantage in developing a global mindset, given that he had crossed borders early in his life, and both his native and adopted countries maintain high education standards, high rates of multilingualism, and easy access, at least in the case of Norway, to the major cultural and business centers of Europe. Yet a global mindset can grow out of much humbler origins than the pan-Scandinavian world that von Tetzchner inhabits.

For instance, global leader Chuck Feeney grew up during the Great Depression in a working-class neighborhood of New Jersey. After serving in the U.S. armed forces during the Korean War, he paid his way through Cornell University by running a sandwich business out of his dorm room.

After graduation, he moved to Europe and ended up on the southern coast of France, teaching swimming lessons as a camp counselor. There he saw an opportunity to sell duty-free alcohol to American sailors who came into port on their way back to the States. His duty-free business eventually grew into the global behemoth now known as DFS (formerly Duty Free Shoppers), but only after Feeney traveled the world setting up regional businesses and hiring local talent to run them. Superbly chronicled in Conor O'Clery's biography, Feeney's story is one of relentless adaptation to changing national and international contexts and regulations.[16]

Saad Abdul-Latif offers another example of a global mind that developed from a less global background. Abdul-Latif is the CEO of PepsiCo's $6 billion Asia, Middle East, and Africa division, overseeing the company's operations in more than a hundred countries; his territory includes roughly two-thirds of the world's population. Despite his globe-spanning job, Abdul-Latif calls himself "just a guy from the neighborhood," a description that might seem falsely humble if it weren't so true. Abdul-Latif's neighborhood is in East Jerusalem, where his family fled from the West Bank after the Six-Day War in 1967. Tense times meant that Abdul-Latif's exposure to the outside world was extremely limited; there were bans on travel and regular curfews. In important ways, Abdul-Latif's world was just his neighborhood.

Abdul-Latif boarded an airplane for the first time when he was eighteen, flying to Lebanon to enroll at American University of Beirut. After graduation, he took a job in Kuwait in organizational development and human resource management. "That's when I first started meeting people with different languages and different religions," says Abdul-Latif. Shortly after, he decided to come to Thunderbird. There his global mindset stretched further. He points specifically to engaging with thoughtful people about the Israeli-Palestinian conflict as a turning point in developing a global mindset. From those, he learned that it was possible to disagree with friends and colleagues on one of the most emotional issues possible and still live, learn, and work together.

Global Mindset: The Benefits for Business

We made the point in chapter 1 that being global is about more than the success measures traditionally promoted in business culture. Building a global mindset as part of the path toward global leadership is far more about the value that comes from developing yourself to engage and grow within today's environment. Yet, a number of the global leaders we have met, engaged with, and studied over the years can clearly attribute their personal success and the success of their businesses to the active possession of a global mindset.

José Antonio Justino: Turning Around
Johnson & Johnson in Brazil

José Antonio Justino experienced the benefits of a global mindset firsthand when he took the helm as managing director in 2000 at pharmaceutical giant Johnson & Johnson's consumer products division in Brazil (JJCB).[17]

Brazilian born and raised, Justino had worked at Johnson & Johnson (J&J) in the United States early in his career as part of a program for young high-potential leaders, and was later based at the company affiliate in Colombia as a country manager. When he was appointed managing director of JJCB in 2000, the Brazilian affiliate had just lost 20 percent of its market share and 67 percent of its profit. Though JJCB had a long-standing presence in Brazil as a trusted provider of brands like Band-Aid bandages and Cotonete swabs, market share was slipping away fast. Brazil's loosened trade restrictions had allowed more foreign competitors to enter the Brazilian market, including American competitors. JJCB's hierarchical and risk-averse corporate culture hindered its ability to compete in the newly internationalized competitive environment.

In response, Justino led a culture change effort to break down functional silos within the company and to encourage more innovation and proactive, decentralized decision making at all levels of the company, not just from the top. This was not an easy task. Brazilian culture scores high in the "power distance" category of the GLOBE framework. Simply put, this means that average Brazilians tend to treat people senior to them with deference and maintain a formal relationship between leaders and subordinates. At the same time, Brazilians exhibit a high amount of "institutional collectivism" and tend to view individualistic leaders negatively. In short, they view their leaders as senior to them, but they still like to be involved in the decision-making process.

As a Brazilian, Justino knew that he would be most successful if he worked with these cultural expectations, rather than against them. He leveraged his global mindset and took advantage of his intellectual, psychological, and social capital assets.

His psychological capital displayed itself as self-confidence, a willingness to try something new and set goals for his company to achieve. His global intellect—developed through experience working for J&J in the United States and Colombia—allowed him to analyze the new competitive environment in Brazil and identify a strategy that incorporated the new foreign market entrants such as Walmart and Tesco, while still serving the traditional mom-and-pop stores that had been J&J's partners for generations. At the same time, he used his skill in developing social capital to connect with the professionals within the J&J organization. He gathered input during town hall–style meetings and listened to the ideas and concerns of his employees. "He knew everyone on the team and trusted us," said one JJCB R&D manager about Justino's personable style.[18]

Aware that Brazilians possess a low "future orientation," in GLOBE terms, he created a seven-month plan with smaller targets built in, so that the JJCB employees could see the value of his initiative and feel a sense of immediate achievement. Of course, a company cannot be completely turned around in seven months, but the short time frame served as proof that allowed him to gain momentum for the midterm.

It did not take much longer for his effort to bear fruit. After performance stabilized in 2002, over the next three years, JJCB went on to achieve a greater than 10 percent compound annual growth rate (CAGR) in sales and 14 percent CAGR in profit. Cost of goods sold, as well as sales, general, and administrative expenses, fell significantly. An initiative to increase sales in northeast Brazil resulted in a doubling of sales there. As for Justino himself, he was ultimately promoted to head all J&J Latin America consumer products (excluding Brazil), a vote of confidence in his leadership style.

Laura Clise: Reducing Environmental
Impact with Smart Ideas

Another example of a person whose global mindset has brought concrete benefits to her firm is Laura Clise, North American sustainability leader for the French nuclear power giant, Areva. Clise was adopted as a child from South Korea by a binational couple; her mother was of Japanese descent, her father German. Clise has spent much of her adulthood expanding her psychological, intellectual, and social capital through studies, hard-won foreign language skills, and experiences living abroad. These capital-building exercises have collectively helped her develop a global mindset that proves crucial in her role at the frontlines of environmental challenges.

Areva's French headquarters launched an initiative called the Sustainable Innovation Challenge, an in-house effort to motivate employees to propose ideas that would reduce the firm's environmental impact. When Clise received the kickoff video from Paris headquarters, she was impressed with the polished, formal corporate presentation, but she knew that what resonated in France might not motivate people in North America. The campaign eventually produced twelve project nominations. Not bad, but Clise thought the North American region could do better in the next go around. So she reached out to colleagues across North America to help her develop a new version of the video.

The result was an "Americanized" campaign featuring real employees and sports analogies like, "We're going for the gold as we race for a better energy future." One French colleague who saw the video exclaimed, "It's so American!" Exactly. The culturally relevant messaging worked, and project nominations doubled.

Lalit Ahuja: Wearing the "Same Shade of Red" at Target

Clise and Justino were both in a situation in which cultural differences played a strong role that they needed to adjust to or tap into.

Lalit Ahuja, CEO of Target India, has taken the opposite approach by looking for common ground.

Target tapped Ahuja as "employee number one" when the U.S. retail giant decided to build a second corporate headquarters in India. Unlike the vast majority of Western firms doing business in India, Target was not established as an inexpensive offshore option for routine or commoditized activities such as customer service or payroll. Instead, Target India focused on enhancing and expanding the firm's business capabilities in store design, technological capacity and development, and firm operations in areas such as marketing, finance, business intelligence, and analytics.

In the early days of establishing Target in India, Ahuja had a few ideas about what he did *not* want to do. Having spent years establishing Indian operations for both LG Corporation and News Corporation, he had much experience in thinking about cultural difference. "I spent a lot of time managing perceptions and educating people on both sides of the ocean on how to work across cultures," he says. "It was an unproductive effort and ultimately produced work that wasn't always relevant."

Ahuja's approach with Target was very different from the typical approach to international expansion. The emphasis was not on cultural differences and adjusting to them but on creating an organization that shared the same corporate culture as Target's headquarters. When he started at Target, he spent several months traveling extensively in the United States. What he found was that Target itself has a strong corporate culture based on fun and friendliness, but also, as the firm calls it, "speed of life" decisiveness. When he returned to India, Ahuja set out to establish his Indian operations on that foundation of company culture, ensuring that everyone was wearing, as he put it, the "same shade of red." He was helped in the early days by an exchange of personnel between India and the United States. His people could go to the Midwest and be steeped in the company culture as he was; likewise, many U.S. professionals went to India to learn and mentor.

One specific, and highly unusual, example of Ahuja's focus on similarities rather than differences is commonality of titles, responsibilities, and pay grades across Target in the United States and Target India. A manager in India can transfer to the United States and have the same responsibilities and span of control that he or she has in India. The company adjusts pay for managers who move between the two countries, just as many companies do when moving employees from Dallas to New York or London to Brussels: there is a cost-of-living adjustment.

Meanwhile, the work done in India is simply an extension of the work done in the United States. The advantage the company gains from its Indian operation is not low-cost commodity services, but the ability to operate twenty-four hours a day, handing projects back and forth across time zones so that the company gains tremendous speed over competitors. Target India focused on building extensions of headquarters teams in areas such as technology, marketing, store design, and so on.

Ahuja's leadership has contributed not only to Target's top and bottom line but also to illustrating that global differences can produce a race to the top, not just to the bottom. Target India is not without its challenges, but Ahuja is convinced that his approach "saved a lot of time and money and effort because no wheel was reinvented."

Growing Global Psychological Capital

Psychological capital is a mental muscle that needs to be trained. Exposing yourself to cultural diversity and engaging with individuals from different backgrounds is the most effective way to strengthen your global psychological capital. Opportunities to travel or live in places other than where you were born offer the most obvious opportunities to train that muscle, so long as you avoid the comfort and ambiance of the internationalist business lounge and hotel lobby we talked about earlier.

Travel is of course not the only option. The different forms of capital do not exist in isolation, but relate to and strengthen each other. Growing intellectual capital through different means—such as learning a foreign language, as well as seeking opportunities to practice that language with native speakers—encourages increased global psychological capital as well. Language teachers often suggest that a key tool for learning a new language is reading articles or works of literature in the language you are studying and then discussing them. This process exposes you in a rather low-stakes way to different ways of speaking, various points of view, and diverse traditions. We say "low stakes" because it is much more difficult to get fired up in a discussion about a fictional story written in a different language than it is in a discussion about, say, another country's abortion policy. Language classes and other contexts that encourage you to understand, or even argue, another side offer important practice in global psychological capital building.

Organizations can help aspiring leaders train that mental muscle by intentionally building teams with members who come from different places and have varying ways of thinking and distinct viewpoints. As an example, when a new class of students arrives at Thunderbird, we design cohorts and project teams to maximize geographic and cultural diversity. The school also requires that students master at least one non-native language, which we believe equips them with one of the most effective tools for viewing the world through multiple interpretative angles. When we design customized executive education classes for multinational corporations, we also strongly suggest that each group include and involve executives from the firms' international operations.

Growing Global Intellectual Capital

Intellectual capital refers to a person's knowledge and understanding of global culture, history, politics, and business. You acquire global intellectual capital through study, travel, and personal experience. The study part of the process puts a heavy burden on an individual's chosen educational path, both formal and informal, in terms of the course of study they choose and even in the institutions where they matriculate.

Formal education serves an important role, even if it provides only part of the intellectual capital needed for a global mindset. From high school courses in world history and geography to undergraduate or graduate majors in international affairs or business, education can be an effective way to develop intellectual capital. Reading international literature; watching foreign documentaries, films, and media; and visiting museums can also help.

International travel allows people to develop intellectual capital, if they use it to create opportunities to embed themselves in contexts that afford learning. It's never too soon to start. Sam and Brady, the two young sons of Thunderbird associate professor

Richard Ettenson, have been traveling with their dad since they were very young. Born in Australia, with years lived there as well as in France, China, and the United States among others, the boys self-published a book entitled *Knock Knock . . . Where Am I?*, a compendium of sixty-nine puzzles designed to teach children and adults about the countries and cities of the world. Their experience as world travelers at the respective ages of thirteen and eleven gave them the opportunity to develop intellectual capital early on and codify it in a form that others could use.

Firsthand experiences within relevant international contexts contribute the bulk of global intellectual capital necessary to succeed as a global leader.

The executives of Legrand, a France-based manufacturer of products and systems used in electrical installations and information networks, learned this lesson in 2006 during an executive education program in Hyderabad, India, run by Thunderbird professors Kannan Ramaswamy and Michael Moffett. Legrand had recently expanded its business into India and believed that much of its future growth would come from the developing world. Recognizing the need for executives to be equipped as global leaders, the company began a program to increase the hands-on experience of managers in global settings.

As part of the program, participants were assigned to one of four groups for real-world observations: one group went to a Hindu temple, one went to a modern Indian shopping mall, one visited a retail outlet where Legrand products were sold, and the last visited a traditional Indian marketplace. Local drivers dropped off each group at the assigned locations and arranged to pick them up later, but the groups had no translators or local guides.

The group that observed the shopping mall noticed that the store selling Legrand products was small, and their name-brand products were surrounded by many less expensive options. They saw that customers who bought electrical products made small purchases and paid in cash rather than credit. Ramaswamy says he could have told the Legrand executives this information in a classroom, but they would have missed the experience of seeing things firsthand. "You could not have gained that insight sitting in Paris or Geneva," Ramaswamy says.

For these managers, being able to see for themselves how consumers interacted with products was a valuable experience and perhaps an obvious step, but one very easy to overlook. During their careers, each of them had probably spent time watching customers and visiting retail sites, engaging in market and competitive research. But as many professionals progress up the corporate career ladder and become candidates for overseas posts, they often move out of the roles for which such firsthand encounters with customers are common. The instinct to see what is happening from the customer's viewpoint gets lost. Legrand and other companies certainly engage in market research in each of their markets. But the leaders who need a global mindset only see it distilled into reports. They don't see it personally and therefore don't develop or maintain the deep intellectual capital they need to be truly effective global leaders.

The takeaway from the Legrand experience is that those seeking to grow their global intellectual capital need to make conscious efforts to seek out information-rich environments and to engage in exchanges that can facilitate insights into the ways of life and history of a new context.

Visiting a local museum or attending a cultural event may not be a top priority in a loaded business agenda, yet it could be the most productive investment of time.[19]

Growing Global Social Capital

There's an old saying used to describe old boys' networks and highly political environments: "It's not what you know, but who you know." Global leaders frankly need both: global intellectual capital (the what) and global social capital (the who). Global social capital is all about who you know and how well you know them. In this age of social networking platforms, you may be forgiven for equating your social capital with the number of accounts you have or connections you have accepted. Social capital isn't built through the casual interactions that lead to an exchange of business cards or Twitter handles. There's a big difference between being "connected" to someone and being in a social capital–enhancing relationship. The number of Facebook friends, LinkedIn connections, or followers on Twitter might be an indication of social capital, but it is an imperfect one at best. The quality and structure of those connections are far more important for building social capital. Nahapiet and Ghoshal, who provided the definition of social capital we used earlier in the chapter, break social capital down into relational, structural, and cognitive dimensions.[20]

The relational dimension of social capital refers to the quality of each relationship in your network: How frequently do you interact with the people you know? How well do you know them? How well do they know you? How likely would they be to offer advice or a valuable introduction? How trustworthy would their advice be?

The structural dimension refers to the patterns of interconnections among the members of your social network and among the members of their respective networks. Are you at the center of the network, connecting many people who would not otherwise be connected? Or are you at the periphery of a network where everyone you know is connected to everyone else in the network? Are you a gatekeeper of information? Do you sit near the hub or at the periphery?

The cognitive dimension of social capital refers to the ability to communicate with individuals in your network via shared language, meanings, and understandings. As your global social capital grows, it takes an increasing amount of cognitive fluency to maintain communications with a diverse network. But maintaining these connections is vital to building social capital, as well as to enhancing your psychological and intellectual capital.

In recent years, a scientific discipline has emerged to investigate social networks and their impact on career advancement, job mobility, power, influence, and management style. For a global mindset, we need to add a fourth dimension: cultural diversity. Global social capital is a function of the number, structure, and quality of relationships across a variety of cultures.

Our best example of a person with extraordinary global social capital is Barbara Barrett, former U.S. ambassador to Finland, aviator and trained astronaut, hospitality entrepreneur, attorney, corporate director, government official, wife of Craig Barrett (the retired CEO and chairman of Intel), and a devoted friend to us and to many others worldwide. Barrett has traveled in multiple capacities. Every year, she lands in at least a dozen different countries, and at every stop she meets leaders from business and government, as well as philanthropists, social activists, and academics. She hosts international visitors at her home in Arizona or at her Montana hideaway, the award-winning guest ranch resort Triple Creek. Barrett has an enormous number of connections in her social network, but what sets her apart is not the number but the quality and global reach of her connections. She intuitively understands that building social capital requires one to *give generously* without an expectation of reciprocity.

Time spent with Barrett is not *networking*. It is meeting with a friend. We never travel anywhere without meeting a business leader or government official who has a wonderful story to tell about when she shared something or showed her generosity in some small, consequential way.

Barbara and Craig Barrett have been generous donors to institutions of higher education, both Arizona State University and Thunderbird. More important than those monetary donations is the way they share the wealth of their social networks. Thanks to Barrett, Thunderbird has had the opportunity every year to welcome thought leaders from different countries and fields of expertise, from the Dalai Lama to former Secretary of State Condoleezza Rice. Through her support, Craig opened the doors that helped the school establish an exchange program with China's leading engineering university, Tsinghua. With her help, the school has developed relationships with Steve Forbes and Supreme Court Justice Sandra Day O'Connor, and has recruited United Arab Emirates Minister for Foreign Trade Lubna Khalid Al Qasimi to its board. Thunderbird has secured the support of many philanthropists for various programs and has raised the resources and contacts necessary to launch an entrepreneurship training program for women in Afghanistan, Pakistan, Jordan, and other parts of the world, known as Project Artemis (which we will discuss in more detail in chapter 4).

Much of the value Barrett brings comes from her ability to see spontaneous opportunities and make immediate connections. Ángel saw this quality in action in 2007 during a meeting of the World Economic Forum in Dalian, China. While there, he received a text message from Barrett asking where he was.

"China," he typed.

"Where in China?" she responded.

"Dalian Congress Center."

"Can you come by the second floor, main auditorium, center front seats?"

Five minutes later, Ángel and Barrett were talking with Al Qasimi, a mutual friend and Thunderbird trustee, as well as the government delegation from the United Arab Emirates. Together, they made plans for a visit to Dubai that helped establish a fruitful relationship between Thunderbird and Zayed University.

If building social capital in general requires a nontrivial investment in time, as well as the assumption of the risks inherent in any trust-based relationship, the development of *global* social capital is even more costly. Acquiring relationships outside the confines of your home environment requires that you leave that environment or find some way to reach beyond it. Cultivating relationships across cultural lines likewise requires that you not only find a common language of communication, but also develop shared meanings. Finally, you have to tackle innate biases, which make it more difficult to develop trust with individuals who look and act differently from you and with whom you may share fewer common relationships.

Where should you begin? The first step is to diagnose your current status. LinkedIn provides a simple test of the diversity of your professional network. Simply look under "Network Statistics" at the distribution of your connections by location and industry.

A more sophisticated application, InMaps, enables you to graphically depict the topography of your network and its structure and reach.[21] Whatever method you employ, a good place to start assessing your global social capital is to understand its geographic and cultural distribution: How many of your connections are outside your region and nation? Of them, how many are of sufficient quality to be potential sources of reliable, trustworthy advice? How many individuals could you turn to for advice on a specific region of the world or for guidance on a business or career opportunity? How global is the social capital of the individuals you are connected to? Answering these questions provides a good indication of where you need to invest.

If one of your areas of focus is to grow your network, a good way to start is to tap into the networks you already belong to, such as alumni groups. Professional associations and conferences are another option. In all these cases, a shared set of meanings and a professional language will facilitate the cognitive dimension. Building social capital nonetheless takes time, and there are no shortcuts. The most important investment you can make is to add value to the people in your network. Don't start by asking them to help you. Start instead by helping them. Barrett and Ángel's chance meeting in Dalian with the UAE delegation would not have happened without Barrett's skill at improving shared networks by bringing in others. Follow her example and help others make connections that will build their social capital.

Look as well for opportunities to help when you can. On a recent red-eye flight between Qatar and Saudi Arabia, Ángel discovered that the passenger sitting next to him was a Thunderbird graduate, a Palestinian-born resident of Saudi Arabia for twenty-five years. A shared experience with Thunderbird and mutual interest in global business provided an immediate basis of communication. In a few minutes, the two had mapped the intersection of their social networks and identified at least three shared acquaintances. Upon arriving in Dammam, Ángel's fellow traveler helped him deal with immigration officials so he could make his connection.

This alumnus was not seeking anything from Ángel—heads of business schools tend more often to ask alumni for favors than vice versa—but he did an effective job in adding a new connection to his social capital and beginning to cultivate it. Simple contributions like these are the foundation on which quality networks are built.

Global Mindset: Start Early, Repeat Often

Developing a global mindset is a lifelong process of learning, investing, and sustaining. Though some, like Chuck Feeney and Saad Abdul-Latif, began developing their global minds as adults, it's never too early (or too late) to start the process. Early exposure to different cultures that include—indeed, require—social engagement can be an effective way to build the foundations of a global mindset from an early age.

In both our cases, we grew up in monocultural families embedded in rather uniform cultural settings. Ángel comes from suburban Madrid; Gregory was raised in suburban northern California. Both of us had to craft our respective learning journeys through education and experience: Ángel studied modern languages in summer programs in France, England, and Germany and then pursued graduate studies in the United States; Greg studied in Europe and traveled to Mexico.

One generation later, our children have a clear advantage. Ángel married an American, and Gregory a Spaniard. Both our families are bilingual, binational, and bicultural. Our children travel between America and Europe and have friends and relatives in both places. These experiences make them culturally aware but they are not sufficient to develop the global mindset as we have described it.

We consciously plan activities that expand their horizons and stretch their ability. In 2008, for example, Ángel spent the summer in China with his family, where they lived on the Peking University "Beida" campus, took classes in Mandarin, and familiarized themselves with the Chinese way of life. Every day on campus presented new challenges. Small events that are so automatic in Arizona—ordering lunch, getting a cab, taking cash from an ATM—became humbling tests.

One day at lunch, the simple task of ordering water almost defeated Ángel. He tried his best to pronounce the two seemingly simple syllables in the correct tones. After four missed attempts, he began questioning his memory and tried several of the other fifteen possible tone combinations, without success. Ángel's wife and kids started laughing, which didn't help him or the waitress, who was losing patience faster than he was. Taking pity on him, Ángel's daughter Emily looked at the waitress and pronounced the two magic words. Ángel couldn't hear any difference between what she said and what he had said, but her results were very different. The waitress smiled and brought them the water, and Ángel got a renewed view of how much more there always is to learn. Our kids are fortunate that they had the opportunity to start early. But in our view, it is never too late either.

Global Mindset Tools:
Questions to Ask, Steps to Take

We've mentioned a few times in this chapter that the first step to take on your path to developing a global mindset is to diagnose where you are now. Here, we offer some questions you can ask yourself to diagnose your current status, as well as some ideas for actions to begin developing your global psychological, intellectual, and social capital. The suggested actions are all fairly intuitive, but they only help if you do them. We know from personal experience how hard it can be to read a news article or watch a movie (without subtitles) in a foreign language. If you're anything like us, your instinct may be to put it off for another time, when you're less tired or less busy. We hope some of the stories from this chapter inspire you. You'll see the results. For more advice, turn as well to the appendix at the end of the book.

Question: Consider a recent experience you had in a culture different from your own. It might have been a trip abroad or an interaction within a different ethnic or religious community. What patterns of behavior did you see as different from what you're accustomed to? Did you make (or observe someone else making) a faux pas?

Action: Consider what purpose those behaviors serve in that community. Reflect as well on what they tell you about your own culture or your own instinctual ways of behaving.

Question: Do you know any people who seem able to seamlessly interact across cultures or seem comfortable adapting to the expectations and norms of more than one culture? What personal experiences and abilities do you believe allow that person to behave that way?

Action: Become a student of those in your acquaintance with global minds. What do they *do* when interacting with individuals from a different culture, or in a group with representatives from multiple cultures? Do they change their ways of speaking? Their patterns of listening? Their body language or mannerisms?

Question: How adventurous do you believe yourself to be? How adventurous are you compared with other people you know?

Action: If you are unadventurous, try stretching your boundaries. If you are very conservative, start small. Eat a meal from an ethnicity you have never tried before, or if you are experienced with international cuisine, ignore the menu and ask the chef to prepare what he would like to eat. Go on a trip by yourself with no travel partners or tour guides. Take note of how you feel during those experiences.

Question: Are you normally interested in or curious about individuals from different cultures? Do you struggle to understand how people from other nations perceive a given reality, incident, or conflict?

Action: Sensitively seek opportunities to ask people from different cultures about their experiences, opinions, or interpretation of events. Listen to the answer; this is not a debate, it's an opportunity to learn.

Question: How much do you know about the affairs of countries different from your own? When you read a newspaper or listen to the news, what proportion of time do you spend with the international issues? Of the last five books you've read, how many were by foreign authors or referred to events or stories in cultural contexts different from your own? How many foreign movies or foreign television shows have you watched in the last year?

Action: Seek opportunities to learn about different cultures. Read nonfiction books or novels written by authors from other countries. Set your computer home page to a newspaper or other news source from another country. Seek out and watch foreign films; for a start, screen the films nominated for awards from the major world film festivals, including Cannes, San Sebastian, and others.

Question: How many of your acquaintances originally came from another country, speak a different native language, and/or belong to a different ethnicity or religion from your own? If you use LinkedIn, check your network statistics: what percentage of your connections live outside your hometown, state, region, or country?

Action: Get in touch. Geographic distance can damage friendships, even those long held. Reach out through your network and reestablish contact. Seek ways you can help before you ask for the same in return.

CHAPTER 3

Global Entrepreneurship: Creating New Value Through Divergence, Convergence, and Networks

Ken Valvur thought he had a global mindset when he arrived at Thunderbird in 1986. The son of Estonian refugees, Valvur spoke fluent French as well as English. But his first days on campus convinced him that his view wasn't as global as he had thought. In an effort to expand his global intellectual capital, he enrolled in Japanese classes. With his sights on Tokyo's booming financial industry, he built his social and psychological capital during a term spent studying in Japan.

The experience paid off when Valvur began working for Scotiabank and managed to secure a post in Tokyo. While there, inspiration struck: Valvur noticed how small eateries in the financial district accommodated their huge lunch crowds by preparing high-quality, premade box lunches, known as bento boxes. Bento boxes gave customers high-quality food—a requirement in Japan—with some customization and minimal wait time. Valvur thought these same characteristics would play well in his hometown of Toronto.

Valvur returned to Toronto after nearly a decade in Japan and opened Bento Nouveau, a food company that offers high-quality, boxed Japanese lunches. Ironically, his first location was in the lobby of the building where he had formerly worked as an executive.

Valvur's understanding of the demand for a better, faster lunch was dead on. Bento Nouveau soon spread to other buildings and shopping malls. But the big breakthrough came when Bento Nouveau expanded into supermarkets. Today, the firm has three hundred locations across Canada and New York, and the bulk of its business is through supermarkets.

Valvur's efforts to develop a global mindset put him in a position to see and capitalize on a cross-cultural opportunity. That success gave him the opportunity to create new value by bringing a Japanese innovation to North America.

Creating new value across boundaries of various types is the second aspect of being a global leader, what we call global entrepreneurship.

What Is Global Entrepreneurship?

There are almost as many definitions of entrepreneurship in business scholarship as there are inspiring examples of entrepreneurs.

The term derives from the French word for *undertaking*. French economist Jean-Baptiste Say first defined entrepreneurs as creative intermediaries who match capital resources with labor resources. Subsequent definitions of entrepreneurship, including famous examples by John Stuart Mill, Adam Smith, and Joseph Schumpeter, often present entrepreneurs as risk-taking innovators who start new businesses.

Global entrepreneurship, in our view, is at once broader and more strictly defined. We subscribe to the definition penned by our Thunderbird colleague Robert Hisrich: entrepreneurship is the process of applying resources and assuming risks in the creation of new value, with the expectation of receiving some reward. The outcome of an entrepreneurial endeavor can be a new firm, a new product, an extension of an existing product to a new market, or a new policy or program to serve those in need. The resources may be tangible or intangible, human or financial. The risks can be personal or shared, financial, reputational or psychological. And the rewards can be monetary, psychological, or social. (See "Is All Entrepreneurship Social Entrepreneurship?")

Is All Entrepreneurship Social Entrepreneurship?

Few topics are hotter at business schools today than social entrepreneurship—the idea of creating social value alongside or in lieu of financial value. Social entrepreneurship as a concept has taken hold perhaps because there is little agreement about what it is. Can nonprofit activities qualify as entrepreneurship? Can profit making in any form be considered "social"? Some argue that the term is redundant because all businesses provide social value by creating the new products and new jobs society demands.

(continued)

In our view, not all entrepreneurship is social nor does everything going by the name of social entrepreneurship create new value. On the for-profit side, it is perfectly possible to form a profitable business that destroys more social value than it creates. On the nonprofit side, it is much more difficult to solve social problems than it is to solve business problems, and the consequences of missteps can be far-reaching. Nonprofits are not subject to the same transparency and disclosure requirements as for-profit firms, and, as a sector, they have never consistently subjected themselves to objective evaluation to see how well their programs serve their constituents. Those that have invested in evaluations rarely share what they find in a way that others can use. As a result, the strategies most social enterprises adopt do not get the public trial and evaluation that can lead to improvement.

We stand by Hisrich's definition: entrepreneurship boils down to assuming risks, applying resources, and creating *value*. If an effort is not creating value in a new way, then it is not entrepreneurship, social or otherwise. Global entrepreneurs, social or not, are able to leverage their global mindset to build bridges, connect resources, and try new approaches to either seize opportunities or solve problems.

Global entrepreneurship takes place in both the start-ups and in mature firms, but that is not where it ends. Global entrepreneurs also work for university research centers, pushing the boundaries of technology in such industries as renewable energy; they work in foundations seeking new ways to fund social value creation or help nonprofits shape strategy; they work in think tanks, building coalitions for new policy initiatives; they even work in government agencies finding unconventional policies and programs that make government work better.

Global Entrepreneurship in the Social Sector

We made the case in chapter 1 that our globalized world both offers immense global opportunities and presents immense global challenges. Exploiting those opportunities and facing up to those challenges requires action on multiple fronts, not just by for-profit businesses. Nonprofit and government organizations need global entrepreneurs as well. Some have already emerged.

Annie Duflo, the executive director of Innovations for Poverty Action, is one such leader who is helping bring a literacy program created by Indian education nongovernmental organization Pratham to other disadvantaged children around the world. The remedial education program, Balsakhi, trains community members, many of whom have limited education themselves, to become teacher's assistants. Once trained, the assistants or *balsakhis*, work in small groups or one-on-one with low-performing students to reinforce basic literacy skills. A balsakhi, which translates as "child's friend," is far cheaper and more easily found than additional teachers would be. More importantly, they are effective. Economists with the Jameel Poverty Action Lab at MIT (J-PAL) conducted an evaluation that showed the Balsakhi program is one of the most successful and cost-effective approaches available for advancing literacy among poor children.

The Balsakhi program itself is an example of new value created to solve a pervasive problem. Its potential is not limited to India, however. There are many countries that have limited resources to educate their country's children—especially the poorest. When the evidence from J-PAL revealed how well Balsakhi worked, Duflo saw the potential to bring the program to other communities struggling with the same problem. Ghana seemed a prime location, given that, like India, the country struggles to educate the poorest members of its population and has a strong education ministry committed to improvement.

Duflo reached out first to the Ghanaian teachers union. "If you want to do anything in education, you need the teachers on board," she said. They were initially skeptical, but Duflo worked to explain how balsakhis help by decreasing some of the variation in the classroom and allowing teachers to focus their instruction. Then, with the union's support, Duflo worked to convince the Ghanaian Ministry of Education, and assembled a group of global funders to back the project. In January 2011, with support from the Hewlett Foundation and other donors, the Ghanaian pilot of the Teacher Community Assistant Initiative (TCAI) went live.[1]

Three Sources of Value Creation for Global Entrepreneurs: Divergence, Convergence, and Networks

Global entrepreneurs bring together people, ideas, and resources from different parts of the world to create new forms of value. They are not satisfied with simply understanding cultural, institutional, and economic differences across national boundaries; they have a unique passion and ability to turn that understanding into new value. Global entrepreneurs create value in three discrete, often complementary ways, by tapping:

- Divergence

- Convergence

- Networks

Tapping divergence refers to value that takes advantage of differing skills, resources, and demand patterns present in various parts of the world. Tapping convergence, in contrast, refers to commonalities, to the needs or resources that people have everywhere. Tapping networks creates value by connecting people or organizations in otherwise separate settings who can serve one another.

Geography, climate, and culture have long played an enormous role in determining what goods, services, and skills flourish in which areas of the world. Nineteenth-century fur traders had better luck in Alaska than in Florida, for example, while winemakers were more successful in southern France than in Sweden.

Regional differences apply not only to natural resources and native species, but also to the collective skills and expertise that develop in specific regions. Computer manufacturing flourishes in Silicon Valley and shipbuilding on the South Korean coast, for instance, and the success of those industries becomes self-perpetuating, as local people cultivate the skills necessary to participate in available economies. The Netherlands has been known for its diamond cutters because its ports served as a convenient neutral market for Portuguese diamond traders; England became the global leader in textiles because its sheep-friendly geography created the expertise that eventually led to innovations in loom and weaving technology.

When industries build up around existing resources and skills, they reinforce those skills by rewarding those who hold them and/or training a workforce to meet its needs. As native industries become overcrowded or lose competitiveness, entrepreneurs find new ways to redeploy the existing capabilities to other, similar needs and problems, what César Hidalgo and colleagues have called "product spaces."[2] It's quite rare for a country or region to make a successful leap into an industry or skill set that is not somehow connected to what is already in place. That's a lesson that has come slowly to many planned economies where government ministers dream up from scratch ten-year plans for building an industrial base in some random sector. Such plans rarely, if ever, work.

Take Shenzhen, China, as an example. Shenzhen did not start as a major manufacturing center, but as a fishing village. It became a major hub for manufacturing because of its fortuitous location just north of Hong Kong. During the disastrous Great Leap Forward and Cultural Revolution, a steady stream of refugees crossed the border into Hong Kong to earn a living. When Shenzhen became a Special Economic Zone during the era of economic reforms under Deng Xiaoping, the city's entrepreneurs were able to leverage the personal and family relationships that many of them had with Hong Kong (their social capital) to build growth businesses. It was those connections that ultimately made this backwater fishing village into a global powerhouse of technology manufacturing.

Different economic regions follow their own paths. Where they can go depends on where they've been. This process results, in almost all cases, in heterogeneity and diversity of competitive capabilities, institutional arrangements, organizational patterns, and culture. There nonetheless remains a popular notion that information technology—and the rapid information exchange it allows—is creating a world that is flat and homogenous and that will eventually be peppered by substantively similar markets. Despite its popularity, that idea is flawed at best. Mauro Guillén, director of the Lauder Institute at Wharton, argues convincingly that: "Countries and organizations do not gravitate towards a supposedly universal model of economic success and organizational form as they attempt to cope with globalization. Rather, the mutual awareness that globalization entails invites them to be different, namely, to use their unique economic, political and social advantage as leverage in the global market place."[3]

In a disconnected world, every region has to create everything it wants and needs. In a connected world, success depends not on emulating or cloning other regions but on accentuating differences. This is as true for countries as it is for companies, where everyone accepts that success is a factor of competitive differentiation. No one expects Google or Facebook to do the same things in the same way as each other or as, say, Microsoft. It makes no more sense to expect globalization to generate homogeneity of countries and cultures.

Sports offer a useful way to think about global possibilities, since the industry of sport is among the most globalized in the world. Mention *El Clásico* in many countries and the only confusion will be whether you are talking about Real Madrid versus Barcelona, River Plate versus Boca Juniors, or Club America versus Chivas. Argentineans, Brazilians, Ghanaians, and Koreans are all found on the rosters of football clubs in Japan, Qatar, Ukraine, Scotland, and the United States. That's not just in soccer, of course; the roster of the NBA All Star Game now includes Brazilian, German, French, Serbian, and Chinese players. Despite this advanced stage of globalization and cross-border integration, however, the style of play of different teams, leagues, and countries remains intact. Norway does not play the same style as Spain; the United States does not attempt to match Argentina dribble for dribble. All of these countries play to their differences, which essentially means they play to their unique advantages.

This is not to say that convergence is unknown in the global sphere. International travel is making people more welcoming, for example, of foreign customs and cuisine, as the Valvur case clearly shows. A friend who lives in a semirural area in the eastern United States recently told us that his two-year-old son had marched into the kitchen and announced, "I want hummus," a product our friend had never encountered until he was in his thirties, despite having lived in three countries on two continents. Spanish fashion retailer Zara has built an empire on its unique ability to uncover a new fashion trend in Tokyo or New York and turn it into low-priced mass-produced items available in stores around the world. The rollout of the iPhone 4 or the iPad created the same excitement (and waiting lines) in Paris as it did in Chicago.

To describe the transformation under way in the global economy as exclusively a process either of convergence toward similar consumer preferences, technology, skills, work habits, and organizational arrangements or of divergence toward completely dissimilar realities is flawed. Instead, the global economy is evolving in complex patterns, convergent in some ways, while stubbornly divergent in others. A globally minded individual is aware of and sensitive to both the increasing similarities and the increasing differences around the world. A global entrepreneur leverages both in order to create new value.

Tapping Divergence

Global entrepreneurs have tapped into differences in resource availability across geographies—from raw materials to skill sets—since the origins of trade. Economist David Ricardo named the unique skills or resources possessed by one country over another "comparative advantage." Trade between two nations often first creates value for both parties when they can each produce different goods at different opportunity costs. In other words, it is differences, not similarities, that first bring trading parties together.

We referred in the introduction to the Dutch East India Company (or VOC) as the world's first multinational corporation. The VOC is also an example of how the original global behemoth emerged through the tapping of divergence. The Dutch of the seventeenth century had an existing European spice distribution network and a reputation for seafaring; the Javanese had pepper. By matching European demand for spices with Javanese supply, the first multinational company was born. The success does not forgive the method; the VOC abused and exploited the land and people of what is now Indonesia. But tapping divergence more commonly yields, as Ricardo originally pointed out, advantages for both sides.

Tapping Divergence in Labor Cost

Take a modern example—Apple and the iPhone. Apple's iPhone is among the top handsets by market share in the United States, due in no small part to the fact that millions of people can afford one. An iPhone is affordable because Apple has tapped into skills and resources available in abundance in different geographic markets. Those skills allow it to build a product that packs more computing power than a 1970s mainframe into a user-friendly handheld device.

The iPhone is manufactured by Foxconn, a Taiwan-based company in business since 1974. Foxconn's complex in Shenzhen employs 270,000 people to make iPhones and iPads, as well as Hewlett-Packard hardware components, Amazon's Kindle, and other well-known devices sold mostly in the West. Foxconn's operation is just one of many employing the 9 million people who now live in Shenzhen. The manufacturing jobs like those at Foxconn's factories in Shenzhen and elsewhere around China are responsible for lifting more than 150 million people out of poverty in the last decade. (The achievement does not excuse the workers rights' abuses and environmental damages that are occasionally reported from these factories, a topic we'll return to in chapter 4.) Every buyer of an iPhone has benefited as well. Apple and its competitors are able to produce devices that Americans and other wealthy consumers want to use at a price that they can afford, and Foxconn is able to employ more than a quarter of a million Chinese.

Tapping Divergent Skills

The most common way of tapping divergence is pursuing low-cost labor, enabled either by lower salaries or by lower worker-protection standards. As many companies that shifted production to Southeast Asia are finding, however, low labor costs are not a sustainable competitive advantage. Competitors will rapidly converge, and labor will become scarce. As there are more employment opportunities, workers will demand higher wages and better conditions directly from companies, or they will pressure their governments for stricter regulations and better standards enforcement. You can profit by running the race to the bottom, but you won't profit very much or for very long. Those who doubt this process should remember that the United States, and specifically New York City, was once the place manufacturers went to find low-cost labor.

The real, long-term opportunities for tapping divergence come from building on differences in skills and competitive advantage. Lalit Ahuja's effort to grow Target India, discussed in chapter 2, was not driven solely by demand for low-cost labor but by his ability to tap a readily available set of operational skills in a separate time zone, so that Target could achieve a level of operational efficiency that would be impossible if all its people and practices functioned solely in the United States. Making sure that everyone at Target India is the "same shade of red," as Ahuja says, allows the firm to deepen the talent and accentuate the differences that drive profitability.

There are plenty of examples of tapping divergence that aren't based on labor arbitrage. Infosys, the Indian company known predominantly as a powerhouse for providing IT outsourcing to Western companies, is also a major employer in Silicon Valley. Similarly, the global wine market has always been based on the divergence in *terroir* between different regions. Chile, New Zealand, Australia, California, and South Africa, as well as the traditional European producers all have vibrant and flourishing wine industries. We all benefit from the rich variety of wine that has emerged from tapping divergence. The same is true of the emergence of Bollywood and Nollywood, both global entertainment creation powerhouses that serve hundreds of millions of Indian and African customers, respectively, far better than Hollywood does.

Rangina Hamidi, the founder and president of Kandahar Treasure, is tapping global divergence with her efforts to bring beautiful Afghan-created goods to Western buyers. Hamidi was born in Afghanistan and spent her early childhood there, but moved to the United States when her parents relocated the family to Virginia. There was no opportunity to return during the reign of the Taliban, but in 2002, after the Taliban regime fell, Rangina returned to Afghanistan with a specific desire to help Afghan women. Her original idea was to form a nonprofit organization to help women in Kandahar. Inspiration struck when she saw hand-embroidered goods in people's homes. Those goods were made with an intricate form of needlework called *khamak* that is unique to Kandahar and the surrounding area. Clothing such as scarves and wraps, housewares such as pillows and tablecloths, and accessories such as purses and necklaces can all be made with khamak embroidery.

Inspired by the beauty and intricacy of the goods, Hamidi decided to form an enterprise to sell khamak-embroidered goods to Western customers. Hamidi bought the materials, chose the products and patterns that the firm would sell, distributed materials and patterns to artisans in the Kandahar area, and established clear and strict quality-control standards. She also forged connections with Western buyers and distributors. Kandahar Treasure operated under the umbrella of a larger development nonprofit for three years until Hamidi rolled out her business as an independent enterprise. What started as a small effort employing twenty-five artisans has trained more than four hundred women and offered them an opportunity to build their own livelihoods.

Hamidi's instinct to tap divergence was in itself inspired, but the important distinction comes from the global mindset she applied to the venture. She knew that existing limitations on Afghan women's freedom would have brought failure to any effort that required women to leave their homes. Hamidi's genius lies in her choice—her business leverages a unique set of skills that women can practice at home and at their convenience.

The example of Kandahar Treasure shows how capturing divergent value can have a large impact on a small scale. For larger-scale efforts, value creation based on differences across regions often leads to supply-chain innovations—improvements in cost or quality that emerge when firms locate specific links of the supply chain in regions with clear comparative advantage. These improvements have been enabled by efficiencies in cargo transportation by land, air, and sea, and modern technologies that can digitize and transmit information. But it is always a global entrepreneur who sees a new way of creating value by understanding and leveraging differences across regions.

Tapping Convergence

Capitalizing on the differences between geographic regions has led to significant success for many companies. Effective global entrepreneurs also create value by tapping *convergence* as it relates to similarity in product demand between geographies.

Entrepreneurs have tapped into divergence since the beginnings of trade, but tapping convergence is a more recent phenomenon, occurring in line with global trade's postcolonialist spread beyond monopolistic, Western-dominated models like the VOC. Just as Ricardo pointed out the benefits that trade could bring through specialization, Nobel laureate Paul Krugman explained 150 years later how unspecialized trade among converging countries with similar skills produces value. Krugman's research shows how Japan and the United States benefit from the fact that manufacturers in both countries make cars and ship them to buyers in the other. Global entrepreneurs see the opportunities created from countries, markets, and people converging.

Convergence involves the identification of products and solutions for which there is diverse demand. People in places as far-flung as Nairobi and New York City sometimes want the same things, from the quotidian, such as a toothbrush, to the critical, such as antibiotics. Sanitation products from Clorox bleach to Lifebuoy soap are marketed and sold around the world, saving lives and growing revenue for their parent companies.

Convergence can, however, be misleading. While similarities in consumer preferences open the doors for new markets, similarities often mask subtle but important differences that can, and often do, cause a product to flop. Even popular products like the iPhone are not used in the same way around the world. Nathan Washburn and Tom Hunsaker, both management scholars at Thunderbird, have noted that the same product can fulfill very different consumer needs depending on context. "If you've ever watched someone trying to text from an iPhone with one hand while hanging on in a packed Line 1 car in Shanghai, you know why, when it comes to texting, most Chinese prefer to put away their iPhones and pull out their other phones," Washburn and Hunsaker wrote in a *Harvard Business Review* blog post. "In fact, the Chinese slang term for the iPhone is *jieji*, or 'street phone,' which might be better translated as 'dress phone.' It's something you show off, like an expensive watch, when you want to impress. In China, the iPhone is a fashion accessory."[4]

Expansion to new markets requires that you understand consumer preferences in the new region, where demand for an existing product portfolio can be high. If your assessment of the opportunity turns out to be correct, increased demand can lead not only to increased revenues, but to additional economies of scale and, eventually, product innovations that can be of value in the home market or third locations.

Tapping Convergence: Developing Opportunities

So-called base-of-the-pyramid strategies tap convergence in product demand between developed and emerging economies by adapting products, packaging, and distribution to meet the specific purchasing power or distribution infrastructure available in large emerging markets. In the case of Danone in Bangladesh, the firm partnered with microfinance organization Grameen Bank to establish a yogurt business adapted to local limitations in infrastructure and retail.

Grameen Bank itself highlights the opportunities in convergent demand for financial services. Before Mohammed Yunus, the bank's Nobel Prize–winning founder, turned Grameen into a recognizable brand and microfinance into a recognizable industry, it was not commonly believed in the global North that it was possible to provide credit to the poor efficiently and profitably, nor that there was such huge untapped demand among the poor for high-quality financial services. Today, Grameen has profitably served millions of poor people in Bangladesh, where it began, as well as in other countries in Asia, South America, and the Middle East. Taking Yunus's lead, global entrepreneurs at nonprofit and for-profit firms have quickly scaled microfinance in dozens of countries. The initial public offering of Compartamos, a Mexican microfinance firm, was one of the most successful of 2008. Globally, tens of billions of dollars have been invested in microfinance over the last decade.

The iPhone has benefited as much from convergence as it has from divergence. Apple leverages the skills and low-cost labor in China to fulfill demand in the United States and other countries of the West; this demand alone has made the iPhone a successful product, with 145 million units sold and counting. But iPhone's marketers are also tapping into convergence by targeting a market position among China's 700 million mobile users. With a market of that size, even 1 percent market share would translate into significant revenue, and new consumer insights will no doubt help Apple better serve the specific needs of the Chinese consumer. Since Apple already manufactures the product in the region, it is simply leveraging existing infrastructure to fulfill a wider source of demand.[5]

Customization and Tapping Convergence

Because of their global mindset capital, successful global entrepreneurs know that convergence in demand rarely means that a product can be brought and marketed unchanged into a new geographic region. Instead, they need to adjust it to appeal to regional tastes and idiosyncrasies and limitations. Yunus did not offer the same credit product to the poor as banks were offering to affluent borrowers. Instead, he adapted it and its delivery to accommodate the uncertain risk of lending to customers without collateral.

One firm that has been hugely successful at adapting its approach to tap convergence is McDonald's. For many, the McDonald's brand conjures images of beef hamburgers and French fries. But McDonald's strength lies not in its ability to produce a stereotypical American menu, but in the consistency with which it serves its customers. The world over, customers want the same thing: a fast, affordable, clean place to get a meal predictable in taste and quality. McDonald's delivers that convergent value, but with menu items that appeal to local culinary culture.

John Quelch, a former professor of marketing at Harvard Business School and current dean of the China Europe International Business School in Shanghai, has written about McDonald's strict strategy of localization in every region in which it operates.[6] As Quelch notes, McDonald's ensures that every restaurant is similar to every other around the world, but since McDonald's is a franchise, the firm also makes certain that each outlet is owned by a local businessperson.

Local ownership ensures that McDonald's is approaching each new location with a global mindset. Thunderbird professor Kishore Dash, who researched McDonald's strategy in India, has shown how McDonald's local owners and management talent allow it to address cultural and religious sensitivities. McDonald's encourages owners to invest in the communities they serve by sponsoring sports teams or other community endeavors. This gives each McDonald's restaurant an unmistakably local feel and creates a visible commitment to social responsibility initiatives. Given the unique cultural space of India, where most people prefer vegetarian foods, and where people's food habits are dominated by regional food preferences, it was not obvious how an American hamburger chain could make it. Yet it did.[7]

Overestimating Convergence: An Entrepreneurial Risk

Tapping convergence in demand across geographies is not simple. There are many cross-border opportunities, but businesses whose experiences are grounded in the preferences of one region have an ingrained tendency to overestimate customer demand, locally and globally, for their products and approach elsewhere. Even when the demand is there, it can be difficult to identify the shifts in business model or pricing that may be necessary in other markets. McDonald's saw that the value it provided was consistency of delivery.

Walmart is in the process of learning some similar lessons about where it can bring value through convergence. Since the late 1990s, the big-box retailer has worked to expand its international presence on the assumption that consumers everywhere want inexpensive goods. When Walmart put this idea to the test in Brazil, it replicated its U.S. approach almost exactly, with large retail spaces and deep discounts. It quickly became clear, however, that Brazil is not America: U.S. prices stay low in part because Walmart can buy in such huge bulk and in part because the firm has invested in state-of-the-art stock and logistics management systems that allow it to optimally balance supply and demand with warehousing and delivery. Those strengths are relatively useless in Brazil, because Brazilian customers prefer local products, and the sprawl of Brazil's major cities makes warehouse-sized spaces impossible to find in high-traffic locales.

Reconsidering its approach, Walmart acquired two local retailers and shifted its local model to operate in smaller stores stocked with local products. Its prices may not be the lowest in Brazil, but Walmart's growth in the region is in the double digits, outpacing the Brazilian market. Some of the insights it has learned in Brazil— such as a model for wholesale supply stores—are now informing its approach in other geographies.[8]

Bridging Developing Opportunities Back to Developed Markets

McDonald's and Walmart are both big firms tapping into big markets, but convergence is not a one-way phenomenon. Most examples of convergence are coming from developed world products, services, or companies moving to the developing world, but over time the connections made between developed-world firms and their developing-world partners and subsidiaries are allowing information to flow back. One Laptop per Child may have stumbled for its lack of a global mindset, but the innovations it has pursued in the effort to create a low-cost laptop for the developing world have made Intel and other microchip and computer manufacturers aware of the unmet demand for such a product in developed markets. There is a straight line between the XO and the netbook, which became the fastest-growing category of the laptop market worldwide, and ultimately the tablet computer.

Global entrepreneurs based in developing economies may tap into convergence by acting as "bridgers" to capitalize on the insights learned in developing markets. Our Thunderbird colleagues Nathan Washburn and Tom Hunsaker argue that bridgers identify and test innovations in emerging markets that they can apply and then bring back to developed economies. It was a bridger at Intel who pursued an effort to develop a netbook powered by an Intel chip, and a bridger at GE who came up with the idea for a portable ultrasound machine for developing markets.[9] (See "Bridgers and Boundary Spanners.")

Bridgers and Boundary Spanners

Thunderbird scholars Nathan Washburn and Tom Hunsaker have coined the phrase "global bridger" to describe a person who brings lessons and innovations from offices or subsidiaries in developing countries back to headquarters. In their research of multinationals operating in emerging markets, they have identified a type of manager who has the global social capital to establish and maintain trusting relationships in subsidiaries and at headquarters, and who has the global intellectual capital to understand the reality of the emerging markets and identify new sources of value to bring back home.[a]

Management scholars normally refer to this crucial role of creating value across borders as "boundary spanning," though the focus of boundary spanning is more multidirectional. Our colleague Andreas Schötter has studied the often-tense relationships between headquarters and subsidiaries in multinational organizations. His work, done in collaboration with Paul

(continued)

Beamish from the University of Ontario, defines boundary spanners as managers who advocate for the best solution to meet the needs of both sides. Boundary spanners "push back toward headquarters when an initiative does not make sense for a subsidiary or the company overall. But they also push back toward subsidiaries when a corporate intitiative has the potential to make the network stronger."[b]

To be effective, boundary spanners must possess a high level of functional knowledge and legitimacy in their organizations. But equally importantly, they must have a high level of social capital at headquarters and at the subsidiary level. "They have networks. People know and trust them at both levels," Schötter says. Multinational organizations need bridgers and boundary spanners as economic power shifts east toward emerging markets such as India, China, and Indonesia.

a. Nathan Washburn and B. Tom Hunsaker, "Finding Great Ideas in Emerging Markets: Why Your Managers Need to Double as Idea Scouts," *Harvard Business Review*, September 2011.
b. Andreas Schötter, "Intra-Organizational Knowledge Exchange: An Examination of Reverse-Capability Transfer in Multinational Corporations," *Journal of Intellectual Capital* 10, no. 1 (2009): 149-164.

The need for bridgers makes clear that the best ideas do not always come from the headquarters office—or from any office, for that matter. A young man from Malawi named William Kamkwamba offers a humbling example of what can happen when you match intelligence, need, and resourcefulness. Kamkwamba lives in a village far from the national electrical grid. Based on a description in an old library book, Kamkwamba built an electricity-generating windmill out of spare parts and trash. His story, now widely known because of a best-selling book, has helped reinvigorate efforts to develop affordable household windmills in the developed world.[10]

A similar story is playing out with all sorts of power-saving technologies developed for countries without reliable electric power. These inventions are finding profitable markets in developed countries because of their ability to dramatically cut energy usage and thereby reduce greenhouse gas emissions.

Tapping Networks

In addition to tapping divergence to optimize supply chains or create unique products, and tapping convergence to capitalize on cross-border opportunities, global entrepreneurs can create value by building and tapping global networks. Network-based businesses build platforms that connect people or organizations so that they can bring value to one another.

The value that networks create accelerates the more people are connected to it. During the dot-com boom, electrical engineer and thought leader Robert Metcalfe described the phenomenon that came to be known as Metcalfe's Law, which states that the value of a communications network is proportional to the square of the number of connected users. Each additional node of a communications network dramatically expands the number of possible connections. For instance, two telephones can only make one connection, but five telephones can make ten connections and ten phones can make forty-five connections. Metcalfe was specifically talking about telecommunications, but the same is true of any infrastructural network. Extending a railway to a new town or adding a new route in an airline network expand value in a dramatic way.

A number of industries benefit from such network economics. They include retail banks, which connect depositors and borrowers with complementary financial needs; insurance companies, which help individuals manage risks through shared, pooled commitments; and online marketplaces like eBay, which connect individual buyers and sellers.

Global entrepreneurs create value by tapping networks with diversely located participants. Take American Express's travel services: the perceived value Amex offices offer is high because you can find one almost anywhere in the world. Customers know that wherever they are, they will be able to exchange traveler's checks for cash, make or change reservations, and, most importantly, replace a lost or stolen Amex card. American Express has achieved this success through independent brand building; airline travel partnerships such as Oneworld or Star Alliance do something similar through collaboration. Each additional partner dramatically improves the value of the network by increasing the number of places a traveler can get to easily.

Networks also create opportunities for independent developers to leverage a common platform. The iPhone's success is built on the global prevalence of the GSM network. Apple in turn has created a new value-creating network through its App Store.

Just as the iPhone taps into a global telecommunications network to transmit the data and content that make it such a useful tool, global entrepreneurs tap into existing networks to find partners, access resources, gather information, find divergence and convergence, and more.

Government's Role in Network Creation

Governments and international organizations often play a critical role in enabling network-based businesses by creating and endorsing international standards in communications, transport, currency exchanges, and systems of measurement and trade, among others. Examples include the telecommunications standard of the International Telecommunications Union, the loose regulations of the nonprofit Internet Society (ISOC), or trade regulations under the World Trade Organization. Other de facto standards have emerged from dominant, privately owned platforms, such as Microsoft Windows or the iPhone, or from distributed open-source efforts such as Linux, which have helped multiply the network-effect incentives for software developers worldwide. Standards, whether de facto or de jure, enable network businesses, but it is entrepreneurs who leverage those standards and connect the right parties in the right way.

Building Networks for Global Value

A good example of a successful global entrepreneur who created value by tapping networks is Merle Hinrichs, founder of Global Sources, a firm that connects Asian suppliers and Western clients to facilitate global trade. Hinrichs grew up on a farm in rural Nebraska, an unlikely background for the development of a global mindset, let alone a global entrepreneurship vocation. But his story is also classically entrepreneurial, complete with a few failed starts. Hinrichs traveled to Japan in the 1960s and started several ventures, none of which went very far. Eventually he settled in Hong Kong. Reflecting on his failures, he realized that he had seen opportunities from convergence and divergence between East and West, but he'd had no network with which to realize them. At the time, there were few connections between the West and East: Nixon had not yet made his historic trip to China, Toyota was not exporting cars to the United States, South Korea was still a developing country, and India was a closed economy.

Hinrichs created a network that would allow entrepreneurs to successfully tap the divergence and convergence opportunities among the United States, Europe, and Asia. In those dark days before the Internet, when international phone calls were more precious than gold, Hinrichs started a hybrid catalogue-magazine designed to help Western companies engage Asian companies as part of their supply chain. A big part of Hinrichs's job was convincing fledging Asian manufacturers to join his network, which he named Asian Sources. Success was self-reinforcing. As more companies signed on, more connected to make deals, and more of those deals produced value for the participants. The word got out and still more firms wanted to join.

Global Sources is now the largest portal brokering connections between Western firms and manufacturers in China. The network that Global Sources has created has been tapped by tens of thousands of firms to create new value.

Another skilled network creator is Linda Rottenberg, founder of Endeavor Global. Endeavor is a nonprofit that cultivates entrepreneurs in the developing world. Rottenberg has tapped her own extensive network of successful developed world business leaders, investment bankers, investors, and attorneys to provide mentoring and coaching to these entrepreneurs. They, in turn, help the entrepreneurs tap global networks to improve and expand their businesses. By the end of 2010, more than 500 entrepreneurs coached by Endeavor were generating $3.5 billion in revenue and employing 130,000 people.

Building Networks Across Borders and Regulations

As global markets grow increasingly interconnected, new opportunities arise to build network platforms that cut across national boundaries and therefore multiply the value for each member. There are nonetheless regulatory and cultural challenges that arise when extending a network beyond the confines of one jurisdiction.

Canada's Research In Motion, the creator of the BlackBerry, struggled in the summer of 2010 to maintain business in Saudi Arabia, the United Arab Emirates, and India after each of those governments threatened to block the popular mobile e-mail service on grounds of national security. Facebook, the world's most popular social networking platform, has run up against a dominant local rival in Spain called Tuenti. The Spanish firm has done a better job of understanding and responding to the preferences of Spanish users. While Facebook eventually caught up with Tuenti, the value of local adaptation Tuenti offers allowed it to hold off a global network that is more than forty times larger.

Networks That Stick

The glue that keeps any network together is trust. Buyers on eBay need to trust that sellers will deliver the promised goods. Depositors need to trust that their banks will have the necessary liquidity to meet unexpected needs for cash. E-mail or voice telecommunications users need to trust that their conversations are secure, and so on. Successful global network businesses like eBay have built trust through a distributed system of ratings. Global Sources built trust in its supplier network by ensuring that every supplier goes through an assessment and a six-star supplier ranking system.

Consulting firms such as Accenture or McKinsey or search firms such as Egon Zender or Heidrick & Struggles have built trusted global advisory networks by developing expertise and local presence in markets worldwide, guaranteeing the same high-quality service in all locations and building sophisticated internal platforms for talent allocation and knowledge exchange. Every new office increases the value offered by any existing office, because every new one increases the range, depth of expertise, and availability of specialized talent. Ironically, the importance of trust in building a network-based business was made dramatically clear by Accenture's now-defunct former parent Arthur Andersen, a legendary global accounting firm that imploded because of its role in the Enron and Waste Management debacles.

Divergence + Convergence + Networks

All of our examples show entrepreneurs tapping independently into divergence, convergence, or networks. These different forms of value are not mutually exclusive, however. On the contrary, some of the most high-potential, high-impact opportunities and solutions involve simultaneously tapping into multiple forms of value—or all three at once.

Murad Al-Katib: Global Agricultural Entrepreneur

Consider the case of Murad Al-Katib and his food trade business in Canada. Regina, Saskatchewan, the heart of the Canadian prairie, probably wouldn't be first on the list of places you would start the search for a global opportunity, but that is where Al-Katib found one.

Canada's western prairie has long been one of the world's breadbaskets, growing and exporting wheat around the world. The global trade in grains has created a vast network in agribusiness, but it has also created problems by encouraging large-scale farmers to grow only one major crop, a practice that leaves participating farmers vulnerable to global gluts and other supply disruptions. While traveling the world promoting Saskatchewan's agricultural trade, Al-Katib noticed that people in many areas prefer what are known as pulses (peas, lentils, beans, chickpeas, and so on) to wheat. Saskatchewan's soil and climate were ideally suited to growing pulses in rotation with wheat, since pulses naturally fix nitrogen in the soil and organically replenish fertility. Farmers that rotate pulse crops with grains have less need for chemical fertilizers or for multiple seasons during which they let land lie fallow. That was convergence. Al-Katib noticed divergence in the fact that Canada has ample prairie land and farmers eager to diversify, while countries that consume lots of pulses have little available land and water.

These observations led to the birth of Alliance Grain Traders, now the world's biggest lentil processor and exporter. Al-Katib tapped into the strong existing networks between Saskatchewan's wheat farmers and the global agriculture trade. He has even leveraged Canada's well-developed network of crop researchers. Scientists at the University of Saskatchewan have developed strains of various pulse crops that ripen quickly so that they perform better in the relatively short growing season in Saskatchewan. Today Alliance operates processing plants and distribution operations not only in Canada, but also in the United States, Turkey, and Australia.

Shai Agassi: Saving the Planet One Car at a Time

Better Place founder Shai Agassi, a leader we introduced in chapter 1, is another global entrepreneur tapping simultaneously into convergence, divergence, and networks to revolutionize the personal transportation industry.

The idea for Agassi's firm, Better Place, arose during a meeting of the Young Global Leaders at the 2005 World Economic Forum in Davos, where former U.S. Vice President Al Gore screened an uncut version of what would become his Oscar-winning film, *An Inconvenient Truth.* The film focuses on the environmental damage that convergent demand for fossil fuels is causing. Transportation accounts for 20 percent of world fossil fuel consumption, a number that is likely to rise as more Chinese and Indians join the middle classes, creating equally convergent demand for personal transportation. Challenged by Gore to come up with a way to reduce fossil fuel consumption within this world of increased convergence, a group of Young Global Leaders considered an alternative model for personal transport. From this challenge of convergence came the germ of the idea for Better Place.

Agassi's firm is not an automaker. Better Place is an auto innovator. The firm is working one country, one battery-swapping station, even one car at a time to replace incumbent, gasoline-powered cars with cleaner electric technology. Better Place may exist because of convergent demand for cars and fuel, but its focused approach is based upon a divergent view of both the world automotive market and the individual drivers who populate it.

Divergence in the world market brought Agassi first to Israel and Denmark, countries that, for very different reasons, are aggressively working to dramatically reduce their reliance on fossil fuels. Israel is motivated by a desire to be independent of its oil-rich neighbors; Denmark, by an environmentally conscious culture and a long-term view of its national economic and environmental health that depends on renewable energy sources.

For the divergent customer, Agassi's aims are high. He is not targeting people whose second vehicle is a bike, or who drive a diesel engine converted to use recycled vegetable oil as fuel. Those people have already reduced their consumption, so convincing them— even becoming their car of choice—won't make the impact Agassi wants. Instead, Better Place targets high-mileage drivers of conventional vehicles, people who cover fourteen thousand or more miles in a year. That segment represents, Agassi says, 25 percent of the driving public but 50 percent of the consumed gasoline.

Convincing that segment en masse to adopt an electric car requires a good-to-great driving experience and convenience, since high-volume drivers spend a lot of time in their cars. Better Place partnered with Renault-Nissan to build the first cars that run under the Better Place banner. The Renault Fluence Z.E. cars are designed to travel longer distances than the seventy-five miles that Nissan's LEAF can travel on a single charge. The Fluence Z.E. is also priced below $20,000, to help consumers avoid the upfront expense and compromises built into GM's Chevy Volt, which carries the price tag of a luxury car yet converts to a gasoline engine when the battery runs out. Last, the Renault Fluence Z.E. was designed with style. "What most people don't get," Agassi says about the Toyota Prius, "is that you're buying a $32,000 Corolla . . . I'm not selling you an alternative to a Corolla. I'm giving you an Audi A6 for the price of a Corolla. That's a very different experience."[11]

There is an argument to be made that Toyota, GM, and Nissan are also creating new value through convergence and divergence with their hybrid and electric technologies. They are addressing convergent demand for fuels and transportation and divergent customer behaviors around environmental consciousness and price points. The Better Place difference lies, however, in its uncompromising focus on creating the network of battery-swapping stations necessary to allow the cars to travel long distances conveniently. The other auto manufacturers are bypassing the network challenge by building hybrids, building gasoline engines within the electric car, or simply putting the onus on the customer to drive only in a very limited range. Agassi wants to do better. He is working with partner governments to build battery-swapping stations that allow drivers to switch batteries in the same amount of time it takes to refuel. The network aspect is such a critical part of the Better Place strategy that it is built into the business model: drivers buy the car, but Better Place owns the battery, which it will lease for a fixed monthly cost, swapping included.

The jury is still out on whether Agassi will succeed in converting millions of high-mileage drivers to electric cars. Success, however, starts with vision. Agassi's has changed the discussion about what an electric model can be.

Identifying Entrepreneurs: Tapping Convergence, Divergence, and Networks in Finance

Both Al-Katib and Agassi have had some advantages in their pursuit of business success: both men work in developed economies where the networks exist to access finance and their personal histories and entrepreneurial skill can be vetted. Unfortunately, millions of developing-world businesses can't get the funding they need because there is no easy way for banks to evaluate them.

The entrepreneurs at the Entrepreneurial Finance Lab (EFL) are tackling that problem by tapping convergence, divergence, and networks in the provision of finance.

The EFL grew out of research by Bailey Klinger and Asim Khwaja, development economists at Harvard, who in 2006 were working together in South Africa on a project assessing ways that small and medium-sized enterprises (SMEs) access capital. They found, in brief, that they don't. In South Africa and throughout much of the developing world, SMEs are locked out of financing networks.

Developing-world banks don't extend loans to small enterprises in volume because there is no easy way for them to assess the risk the borrower presents. Even in South Africa, which has a robust and mature financial sector compared with most developing countries, there are no systems like Equifax and Fair Isaac in place to capture financial data on individuals and convert that data into a credit score that banks can use to make lending decisions. Assessing each small business and business owner on a case-by-case basis is not really an option. For these relatively small loans, the cost of due diligence would easily overwhelm any profits. As a result, developing-world SMEs often cannot access growth capital. This lack of financial access is one of the main reasons that few developing countries have a robust SME sector. This "missing middle" means fewer jobs, fewer opportunities, fewer trading partners, fewer firms contributing to growth and GDP, and so on.

Klinger and Khwaja wondered if they could build a tool to generate a risk score for an applicant based on a few pieces of easily attainable information. They considered a few alternatives in their search for an ideal tool: they looked at lie detector tests, personality tests, game theory, and statistics. They ultimately decided to adapt the psychographic tools that human resource departments in large firms often use to assess potential candidates. Klinger and Khwaja adapted these psychometric surveys to focus on a variety of factors that would likely have an impact on loan repayment, such as intelligence, honesty, and diligence. They then tested the tool over three years with thousands of applicants at banks in Peru, Colombia, Kenya, and South Africa.

The results of those tests revealed another fascinating example of convergence. The psychographic factors that influence repayment are fairly constant across cultures; in other words, the same traits that make a South African trader a good credit risk also make a Peruvian weaver a good credit risk. While there are some necessary adjustments for how culture affects scores on various dimensions, the basics are the same the world over.

It's one thing to conceive of an idea that works in theory, and yet another to put that idea in practice and see it work so well in the real world that banks deploy it widely. That's exactly what EFL has achieved. Tests in the field conducted with banks that used the tool to make credit decisions showed that the EFL psychometric analysis outperformed the judgments of loan officers, significantly cutting default risk on the small business loans.

That success is allowing EFL to tap the existing networks of banks to deploy the tool and use it to address the credit gap for SMEs worldwide. Standard Bank, based in South Africa and one of the original testers of the EFL tool, is now rolling out the EFL approach in the seventeen countries it serves in Africa. The bank estimates that it will make more than $1 billion of loans to SMEs over the next few years using EFL's test.

Interestingly, EFL is organized as a for-profit, though it was definitely founded to confront a social problem. Klinger says, "If you care about scale, about reaching the small and medium-sized enterprises, then it needs to be profitable for the people who have the money—the banks. We were getting great support from donors, but we needed to have a business structure if we were going to be taken seriously." EFL is now being taken seriously based on its results; banks not only in Africa but in Latin America are putting their money on the line with the EFL methodology.

Growing Global Entrepreneurship Skills

Robert Hisrich, mentioned earlier, believes that some of the most effective entrepreneurial thinking comes by combining the processes of causation and effectuation. Hisrich often cites the work of University of Virginia Professor Saras Sarasvathy, who compares these two approaches to cooking. A causation process requires the cook to plan dinner, identify the recipes, shop for ingredients, and then cook the meal. An effectuation process starts by assessing the ingredients and utensils at one's disposal and then deciding the menu around what is feasible. Effective entrepreneurs use a combination of both causal and effectual thinking, depending on the context.

How do aspiring entrepreneurs develop their causal and effectual thinking skills? Causal thinking requires a global entrepreneur to develop strong analytical skills in all areas of business administration—marketing and strategy, finance, accounting, human resources, and operations and project management—all with a global dimension. Most business programs or on-the-job training offer these skills from an ethnocentric perspective based on the culture in which they are based. Business schools that acknowledge the increasing global context then add a specific course in international business to tweak the basic skill sets to work on an international scale.

Some leaders do just fine with this model, particularly those that have been exposed to multiple cultures and so have a head start in developing their global psychological, intellectual, and social capital. We nonetheless recommend a more embedded approach, one that considers a global dimension in every business discipline so that people develop analytical skills within the complex context in which they will need to apply them. Classes at Thunderbird are designed with this embedded view in mind, and it follows through in the cases and readings students analyze.

Global entrepreneurs must also be equipped to think through an effectuation process, that is, to develop an increased awareness of the assets at their disposal for the creation of new forms of value. Recall that Klinger and Khwaja did not try to invent a tool from nothing, but instead looked to parallel sectors like psychology, law enforcement, and gaming for ideas and input. They wanted to see what was there already and what they could use. Agassi also looked at what was already available, but the biggest lessons he took from the Prius, the incumbent green automotive technology, informed him more fully about what he *didn't* want to do.

Whether following a causal process, an effectuation process, or some combination in pursuing opportunities to tap divergence, convergence, or networks, global entrepreneurs are always served by their global mindsets. Understanding relevant differences across multiple geographies is critical for tapping divergence, understanding commonalities across markets is critical to expand to new markets and tap convergence, and cultivating strong personal social capital is critical both to tap networks as well as to build partnerships that allow an idea to grow.

Global Entrepreneurship Tools: Questions to Ask, Steps to Take

As in developing a global mindset, the first step to take when developing your global entrepreneurial skill is to assess where you are today. How skilled are you at thinking through and identifying entrepreneurial opportunities? Here are some questions to ask yourself to assess your present state, along with some recommendations for actions you can take to develop your entrepreneurial skills for identifying opportunities to tap divergence, convergence, and networks. See the appendix as well for more ideas.

Question: What products and services do you consume in the course of a day that are produced, either in whole or in part, by an organization that is not based in your home country? Probe your knowledge. Are these products the same everywhere they are sold, or did they have to be adapted for your market?

Action: Identify three successful products a foreign firm introduced into your home market. Are these products examples of the provider taking advantage of divergence, convergence, or networks? Find three products that foreign organizations introduced into your home market that did *not* succeed. Analyze why they failed.

Question: Do you know any "global bridgers" or "boundary spanners" in your organization? What do they do to be successful in their role?

Action: Become a student of a global bridger. Try to learn about the key skills those individuals use to succeed in their role. Watch and learn what they do. How do they learn what they need to know from their subsidiaries and how do they sell good ideas at headquarters?

Question: Are there any organizations in your industry that have expanded to new markets to take advantage of convergence in customer preferences? What business models are they adopting? Are they successful?

Action: Choose a country where your company does not have a presence—any one will do—and see what you can find out about the state of your industry in that country. Are there existing companies that do just what you do and produce products just like yours? If so, try to find some ways in which they are both similar to your firm and different from your firm. What would it take for a new firm to compete with the incumbent?

———————————

Question: Do you know any firms in your industry that have improved their efficiency, costs, or innovation capability by relocating parts of their supply chain in a different location?

Action: Consider the key factors in that firm's success. What did it have to do to gain those efficiencies? Is the improvement replicable by another firm?

———————————

Question: Do you know of any organizations that have built new global networks to serve customers or enable customers to provide value to one another? What was the key to their success?

Action: Networks are really about connecting parts of a system to each other. Make a list of the networks that your firm or your industry is missing and that could help improve efficiency, costs, or even your ability to capture new customers. Consider what it would take to build them.

Question: A huge percentage of start-ups fail to survive for more than a few years, but their founders often go on to start a successful company later. Do you know an entrepreneur who has experienced both success and failure with a start-up?

Action: Find a serial entrepreneur who has both failed and succeeded. Learn more about their story and analyze what role divergence, convergence, and networks played in each of their entrepreneurial attempts. Could global entrepreneurship skills have salvaged a failure or accelerated a success? How?

CHAPTER 4

Global Citizenship: Contributing to Prosperity and Value for All

A few years ago, a group of Thunderbird faculty members, students, and alumni set out to identify the leader who best exemplified the school's values. After a long debate, the group was deadlocked. A single person couldn't capture Thunderbird's values. The school had a split personality, exemplified by two very different individuals: Richard Branson and the Dalai Lama.

Branson seemed an obvious choice. A self-made billionaire and *über*entrepreneur, the well-known Briton has grown a highly profitable global brand from industries once considered moribund. The Dalai Lama felt like more of a stretch. What does a Tibetan monk have to offer as a model for a business school? Turned out, he had the answer a few months later, in September of 2005, when he visited Thunderbird. In his speech, the Dalai Lama spoke about individual responsibility in an interconnected world:

> We are more than six billion people and we are suffering from complex global problems, many of them man-made. The world is one unit, one body, but our minds still think in terms of *we* and *they*. In reality, however, there is no such thing as *us* and *them*. We are one body. So the destruction of one part is the destruction of the whole. We must make an effort to recognize that the "others" are also part of humanity, that my future depends on your future. We may find some comfort in the notion of independence, the idea that we control our destiny and can take care of ourselves, but that idea only exists in our mind. In reality, we are all interdependent.[1]

The Dalai Lama described the two central tenets of Buddhism: one involves a philosophical outlook that recognizes the interdependence of all things; the second, a value system based on the notion of compassion and the consequent requirement to cause no harm to others. These two ideas are interconnected. If I believe that I am connected to you, then your pain or hardship is also mine, and it is in my self-interest to do something about it.

What Is Global Citizenship?

The Dalai Lama's ideas about interconnectedness and compassion helped us frame our views on what global citizenship means in a business context.

Global citizenship involves taking actions and making business decisions that recognize the ways in which the prosperity of one individual, one firm, or one nation depend on the prosperity of others. A global citizen is committed to respecting the rights and dignity of all individuals who are affected by his or her business. A global citizen will work at creating true value for all parties involved in a business transaction rather than trying to exploit some for the benefit of others.

The concept of global citizenship is not new. More than twenty-four hundred years ago, the philosopher Socrates claimed: "I am not an Athenian or a Greek, but a citizen of the world." U.S. President Ronald Reagan called himself a "citizen of the United States and of the world" in a speech before the UN General Assembly thirty years ago, and Barack Obama appropriated the phrase in Berlin while still a candidate for the presidency. Socrates, Reagan, and Obama all communicated that they were invested in the larger fate of humanity and that their fate was tied up with that of others.

Global Leaders Need to Be Global Citizens

There are two important arguments for conducting business as a global citizen: one is a moral imperative; the other, a practical one.

The influence they wield and the resources they command oblige global leaders to act as good citizens. Alternatives, of course, abound. Global business is full of legal loopholes and ambiguities. It offers plenty of opportunity for moral arbitrage, for a race to the bottom in which each actor tries to outearn the rest by cutting corners and exploiting weak links. Our definition of global leadership excludes that type of conduct, no matter how much personal gain it may bring. A global leader instead chooses to make decisions and build new sources of value that create prosperity, alleviate poverty, and improve well-being. Achieving those outcomes is a direct function of how leaders understand and act upon their personal responsibility.

True global leaders do not think it is okay to look the other way when their Malaysian outsourcer employs thirteen-year-olds just because regulation is lax or ideas of childhood are different in Southeast Asia than they are in the West. Global leaders view themselves as citizens of all the communities in which they operate and accept responsibility for their impact on the community's welfare. True global leaders reject the all-too-common zero-sum mindset, which sees prosperity as finite and success as a race to take as much of it as possible.

There is increased recognition of the need for leaders to act as global citizens. Global citizenship for leaders is gaining the endorsement of organizations like the United Nations and the World Economic Forum, and has been written about by influential thought leaders like Harvard professor Michael Porter, whose ideas about "shared value" are not very different from our definition of global citizenship.

On the practical side, global citizenship is not just *right*; it is also instrumental to success. Conducting business in any other way is becoming increasingly difficult. Many individuals and businesses allow the rule of law to serve as the far edge of their moral obligation, but laws rarely reside on the cutting edge of need. Governments are slow-moving animals. Standards of behavior today are increasingly set elsewhere—by the shareholders who believe you are putting their investment at risk by not considering the larger picture; by journalists who make that picture clear in their reporting on the working conditions at overseas operations; at the NGOs that investigate corporate relations and behavior; even on the personal blogs, YouTube videos, and Facebook pages of company employees discussing their experiences. Corporate actions used to be a matter private to international boardrooms. Today, increased transparency, often involuntary, means more scrutiny. The world is watching now, all the time.

Not only does global citizenship reduce a leader's risk of failing; it also pays dividends. Our colleagues Mary Sully de Luque and Nathan Washburn demonstrated in an article in *Administrative Science Quarterly* that the followers of CEOs who emphasize good citizenship values perceive them as more visionary than the leaders who are autocratic and focus on economic results at any cost. The article was based on a study de Luque, Washburn, and collaborators conducted with leaders in 520 firms in 17 countries, which found that those leaders displaying citizenship values had a huge influence on their employees; their subordinates exerted additional effort at work and made their companies more successful.[2]

For global leaders, global citizenship is a base requirement. A businessperson may apply a global mindset to perceive, analyze, and decode situations, and he or she might apply a global entrepreneurship to identify opportunities from divergence, convergence, and networks. But using these skills will only make the person a global leader if he or she approaches every situation with the goal of creating shared value for all parties involved.

Global Citizenship: An Uncommon Path to Common Solutions

Many readers at this point may be tallying the number of successful leaders they know in business and politics who do *not* operate as global citizens. Some high-profile thinkers even revel in rejecting the view that strong leadership requires global citizenship. Politician Newt Gingrich, responding to Obama's speech in Berlin, called the concept of global citizenship, "intellectual nonsense and stunningly dangerous."[3] (It's not clear how he felt about Ronald Reagan's use of the phrase.)

The global recession has spurred more than a little economic nationalism in many communities and businesses. You do not need to look far to find examples of businesses behaving badly for short-term gain in places or situations where the risk of reprisal is low: agribusiness giant Chiquita has paid bribes to paramilitaries in Colombia; Nike sourced apparel and other products from factories in Pakistan that employ children as young as ten; food processor Cargill has discouraged the companies it supplies from testing its meat products for *E. coli* bacteria.

It's easy to critique the misbehavior of these corporations. But each situation is more complicated than it might appear. Colombia, for example, has been caught in a three-way conflict between the elected government; a communist guerilla movement that started out as an ideological group and evolved into a kidnapping and extortion racket; and right-wing paramilitaries originally set up to protect people from the guerillas, but have become organized crime and drug-trafficking syndicates. Paying bribes in this context is not necessarily done with overtly corrupt intentions; Chiquita paid the bribes in part to protect its workers from threats of violence from the paramilitaries.[4]

Nike followed the path of many apparel manufacturers and outsourced much of its production to low-cost countries as a way to compete in an extremely price-sensitive market. At first, Nike couldn't understand why the public expected it to police contract factories in far-off lands. Later, when responsibility appeared unavoidable, it asked suppliers to comply with local laws and Nike standards. Nike didn't have the staff, however, to conduct regular audits of all its suppliers (some of whom were outsourced providers for Nike's outsourcers).[5]

Even Cargill had its reasons. The major food processors are constantly challenged to stay competitive while keeping food prices affordable. There are pressures coming from many sides to push up

Cargill's costs, including increased fuel costs, loss of cattle or feed to weather or natural disaster, and fluctuations in demand, among other issues. Food safety is another source of expense, and the outcomes overall are very good; food-borne illness caused by unsanitary practices at the abattoir or processor is very rare. It can be argued that the media pays such close attention when contamination occurs exactly because it is so rare. The necessary investment to make food even safer within the current system would be substantial; removing the last half-percent of error is always vastly more expensive than removing the first 99 percent. The only way to offset the cost would be to make food more expensive, which would put a great deal of pressure on people around the world who already struggle to afford food.[6]

We raise these examples to show that the path to global citizenship is not easy and its rules of engagement are not always obvious. Global leaders confronting these issues often tell us they are the most difficult and complex management challenges they face. Do you pay the paramilitaries or let your employees be kidnapped or murdered? Do you trust the relationships you've established with your business partners or do you spend large sums of money to audit all of them regularly? Do you seek "good enough" protection or establish a higher food-safety standard that makes food less affordable for the poorest consumers?

These situations can seem like catch-22s offering no good choice. Yet they are where global leaders stand out. Global leaders keep the questions and challenges of citizenship front and center for every decision they make, using their mindset and entrepreneurship skills to find a third way—a way that benefits customers, employees, investors, and communities. What's encouraging is that the universe of innovative ways to do business is vast, and global citizens who can find that third option are becoming more common.

Fighting Corruption

A ubiquitous problem facing global leaders operating in a transnational context is corruption. In many countries, government officials expect to receive special treatment from anyone who needs their support. This can be as blatant as handing over an envelope stuffed with cash or as subtle as arranging a well-paid internship for an official's relative. Or it can be masked as professional fees paid to retained local "consultants." The World Bank estimates that $3 trillion every year is misallocated to the personal gain of government officials.

Corruption may seem like a very large-scale, entrenched system whose effects are difficult to influence at the individual level. But even a cursory examination of the well-researched and documented reports on corruption by organizations such as Transparency International, a nongovernmental organization, or the World Bank makes clear that corruption has an enormous effect on the lives of the world's most vulnerable citizens. Nearly all of the countries of the "bottom billion" share the lowest scores in the corruption perceptions index developed by Transparency International (the lower the score, the higher the corruption): Chad, Sudan, Angola, Burma, Turkmenistan, Afghanistan, Somalia, and Iraq.[7] Nigeria, a country that scores a 2.4 on the 10-point index, had by 1990 earned an estimated $300 billion in oil income from the time crude was discovered there in the 1950s. But in that same time, the well-being of the country's populace actually declined. While ordinary Nigerians were losing ground, Nigeria's brutal leader of the late 1990s, General Sani Abacha, retreated to his villa to enjoy the $2 billion to $5 billion he'd taken from his country's bank accounts.

Corruption is not just a scourge of politicians and citizens. It also does great damage to businesses. Corruption can add anywhere between 25 percent and 100 percent to the cost of a project. Standard & Poor's estimates an 80 percent to 100 percent risk of total investment loss in the world's most corrupt countries.

Corruption is clearly a societal scourge, but the options on the ground rarely seem so black-and-white. In environments where companies feel compelled to play along with corrupt leaders, resistance often means lost contracts, lost market share, and lost jobs for employees and suppliers. In these environments, leaders may feel as if resistance is a lonely, thankless pursuit that makes little difference. But emerging global leaders are showing that resistance is not futile.

Global Citizenship in Action

Bill Browder, the founder of the hedge fund Hermitage Capital Management, took on corrupt practices in Russia. Browder moved to Russia in the mid-1990s and started the fund to invest in Russian companies, particularly in the oil and gas industry. Russia at the time presented huge opportunities in an environment with little order; Russian financial markets had been compared to the Wild West. When the fall of communism led to the privatization of state-owned firms, a great deal of corporate value was sold off at fire-sale prices to investors who came to be called *oligarchs*. The oligarchs often ran the companies as vehicles for their personal benefit. Modern corporate governance was practically nonexistent.

Browder's first opportunity to fight this culture of corruption came when the owner of Sidanco, an oil company in the Hermitage portfolio, tried to cash in on gains in the firm's market value by issuing convertible bonds sold at a 97 percent discount to the market price to a select group of insiders. The move would have diluted Hermitage's position by 70 percent and possibly wiped out the fledgling fund.

Browder contacted other shareholders to ask if they would be interested in joining him in a fight to stop the bond issue, which was clearly illegal under Russia's investment laws. Most wanted nothing to do with a conflict in Russia. "People told me, 'This is just the way Russia works,'" and they refused to join the fight, says Browder. But he refused to capitulate. He devised a sophisticated strategy to bring pressure on Sidanco. He began a media campaign to publicize the dilutive bond issue to all investors in Russia, foreign or otherwise. He then publicly pressured the Russian securities regulator to enforce the law and cancel the dilutive issue. With the combination of media pressure and private coaxing of the regulator, Browder's stand ultimately worked, and the Russian authorities ruled the Sidanco bond issue illegal.

The biggest battle for Browder was yet to come. Seeking to clean up other companies in his portfolio, Browder's team began looking at Gazprom, the largest oil and gas firm in Russia. Gazprom's management at the time was known to be extensively corrupt, but no one knew how far the corruption spread. In the face of this uncertainty, the market was valuing Gazprom at a 99.7 percent discount compared with ExxonMobil per barrel of reserves, a signal that the market believed management was stealing nearly all of Gazprom's value. To test the conventional wisdom, Browder assigned his team of financial analysts to conduct a forensic audit of Gazprom's activities to determine how much money was going missing from the company through corruption. Their research uncovered a startling fact: management was "only" stealing about 10 percent of the value of the company. The common wisdom of the marketplace was wrong, and Hermitage increased its stake in Gazprom to make it the largest position in the fund and made its findings public through the *Wall Street Journal*, the *New York Times*, and the *Financial Times*. As a result of the publicity, the government was forced to react, and it conducted its own forensic audit of the company. The Russian Parliament launched its own probe as well; as a result, more than five hundred newspaper articles followed. In the end, the scandal became so intense that Russia's president was forced to fire the CEO and replace him with a new manager. As a result, the share price doubled in the subsequent period, rising nearly one hundred times over the next six years, and Hermitage saw a significant increase in the value of its holdings.

If that were the end of the story, it would hardly be an example of global citizenship. But Browder's intent wasn't just to profit, it was to improve corporate governance and fight corruption so that everyone in Russia, not just investors, would benefit. So Hermitage launched the same type of anticorruption campaign at the national electricity company, the national savings bank, and many other companies. The campaign took several years, but it was also a success. The Russian government ended up changing the law to prevent dilutive share issues at banks, it changed the charter of the electricity company to prevent asset stripping, and it started cracking down on dubious intermediaries in gas exports out of Russia.

Unfortunately, Browder's story in Russia does not have a happy ending. While he won the battle against corruption at a number of companies, he also created powerful enemies. Browder was eventually expelled from Russia and named a threat to national security, a victim of retaliation. Once he was banned from the country, corrupt Russian authorities raided his offices and seized all of his corporate documents to fraudulently take control of his investment companies. They then used the companies to apply for an illegal rebate of $230 million of taxes paid by Hermitage the year before. Hermitage's Russian lawyer, Sergei Magnitsky, discovered the scheme and testified against the corrupt officials involved in the fraud. He was subsequently arrested on trumped-up charges by the same officers he had testified against. He died in jail after being held in appalling conditions and denied medical care for 358 days as these officials tried to get him to retract his testimony.

Browder nonetheless continues the fight. At the 2011 annual meeting of the World Economic Forum, he called attention to the lack of transparency and corruption of Russian officials during a session where Russian president Dmitri Medvedev was speaking. He says, "What motivated me at first was economic interest. When we got into Gazprom and saw how costly it was to the company and the country, it became a fight of moral indignation. We wanted not to just make money but to make Russia a better place. After what they did to Sergei Magnitsky, it is now exclusively a fight for justice."

Meanwhile, Browder has carried his fight against corruption and for better corporate governance to companies and markets around the world. Browder offers a cautionary thought for all leaders about the dangers of not being a global citizen: "If you don't fight corruption, you're not just acquiescing. You become complicit. You are a part of the corruption. Once you cross that line you may be able to make more money, but you can no longer sleep at night."

The Group Effect of Fighting Corruption

For some, the price paid by the Bill Browders of the world—or more saliently, the Sergei Magnitskys—may simply be too high. Why do business at all in environments where the rule of law is weak and unpredictable? There are at least two powerful reasons. First, there are still great opportunities to create value, even in environments that are loosely regulated. Second, responsibly run businesses are a necessary component of a just, prosperous society. By seizing business opportunities rooted in global citizenship values, global leaders can create new value *and* contribute to a better society.

Whatever the motivations, firms of all sizes find it desirable or necessary to work in regions or countries that challenge their ideas of citizenship. GM, for example, pursued a joint venture beginning in 2001 with Russia's largest carmaker, AvtoVAZ, despite concerns over the unpredictability of Russian law. GM's continued growth depended on such expansion. Far from validating corruption, when major stakeholders like GM enter markets with corrupt elements, the way they choose to conduct themselves can create great opportunity for change. It is very difficult, after all, to positively affect a system in which you do not participate.

Global Citizenship at Fluor: Developing PACI

The path for Browder and Magnitsky was made more difficult by the fact that they were in the minority among firms willing to take the risks that are sometimes necessary for a global citizen. Fluor Corporation has taken the different tack of seeking strength in numbers. Fluor is an international *Fortune* 500 construction and engineering firm that serves the oil and gas, petrochemical, and defense industries, building power plants, pipelines, and other infrastructure projects. Fluor is active in more than twenty-five countries.

The construction industry is particularly vulnerable to corruption, largely because the number of contractors and subcontractors and the volume and variety of supplies make it easy for groups to band together to rig bidding, hire shell companies to funnel bribes, and bill for hours not spent or for goods not bought. Transparency International reports that oil and gas, aerospace, and defense are also high-risk fields for corruption.[8] In 2009, for instance, Halliburton agreed to pay $559 million in fines to the U.S. government to settle charges of corruption in Nigeria. In late 2011, *Bloomberg BusinessWeek* published an investigatory series on allegations of corrupt business practices at various subsidiaries of Koch Industries, another major player in oil and gas infrastructure.[9]

Corruption is a complex social cancer because it creates what sociologists refer to as a *social dilemma*. In a social dilemma like corruption, individual actors, that is, those who solicit or give bribes, benefit personally from the behavior, yet the entire community bears the costs. Social dilemmas can be difficult to break because each person in the society figures he or she is better off if complicit regardless of what others do. Each has to bear the societal brunt of corruption, no matter what, so at least by cheating each reaps some personal reward. Sociologists have nonetheless documented several paths to break down social dilemmas, one of which is collective action.

For Fluor, the collective approach gave the firm a way to retaliate after years of being hit for bribes and losing contracts to those willing to play along in a corrupt system.

Fluor board chairman Alan Boeckmann began working with other companies at the World Economic Forum to develop a number of anticorruption principles. As the new kid in the CEOs club at Davos, Boeckmann was elected to lead his sector group. He agreed to the position on one condition: that the group take action on corruption, a problem that was vexing them all. His peers agreed, and their work evolved into the Partnering Against Corruption Initiative (PACI), a pledge that participating firms take to fight corruption in their own ranks. PACI signatories refuse to pay bribes and agree to share anticorruption best practices with other companies. PACI commits signatories to attack the supply side of bribery that they control. Doing so collectively ensures that no one gains unfair advantage in contracts. Call it an anticorruption cartel.

There are now over 145 signatories to PACI, including Coca-Cola, Archer Daniels Midland, De Beers, Siemens AG, UPS, Royal Dutch Shell, and other major international players. PACI operates in cooperation with Transparency International as well as the International Chamber of Commerce and the United Nations Global Compact.

When PACI was first introduced in 2007, 28 percent of the participating companies did not have an anticorruption program in place; at the end of 2009, only 2 percent did not have a program. Fluor, for example, puts all employees through anticorruption training and has set up a hotline to allow employees to report incidents at their sites and get advice on how to handle them. It also requires its business partners to sign on, extending the impact of PACI throughout the supplier network.

PACI also puts teeth into the commitments. In many instances, signatories offering competitive bids against each other for work in corrupt environments enter into what are termed *integrity pacts*. These are binding legal agreements in which each participant promises not to engage in bribery. Failing to live up to the pledge comes with a stiff penalty, like forfeited damages. There have been dozens of these agreements enforced around the world.

Possibly even more relevant is the cooperation that PACI encourages between companies and government officials. When Fluor employees were harassed and arrested after refusing to hire a local firm to provide "security," the local manager sought the help of the regional government. Fluor also signaled in another context that it would not pay bribes to port officials and worked within the region to bring its goods in through other, less convenient methods. By making the announcement and holding to it, Fluor sent a clear message and now passes goods through the port without incident. Those successes have made it possible for Fluor, when it enters into a contract within a country, to enlist the help of the local, regional, and national governments and work with officials to sign an agreement in which the government commits to prosecute any company or official that pays or seeks bribes.

Such creative solutions seem to be catching on. Intel in Vietnam was not a signatory to PACI at the time of this writing. Yet in 2007, it signed a memorandum of understanding with the Saigon Hi-Tech Park that confirmed the parties' mutual agreement to adhere to a set of business ethics and rules of conduct. The idea was to maintain fair competitiveness between Intel and other investors in the Saigon Hi-Tech Park.

At the grassroots level, a number of projects have recently emerged to leverage crowdsourcing and online social networks as a tool against petty corruption. For example, the organization Mi Panama Transparente is using Ushahidi, the mobile crowdsourcing platform, to gather citizens' reports on where they have been victims of corruption or crime. A text message sent to the Ushahidi platform contains information about the location of the interaction, which allows the system to create maps highlighting hotbeds of corrupt activity or crime. When events cluster in a particular location, it becomes increasingly hard for governments or law enforcement to ignore them.

Another example of grassroots anticorruption activity is Vijay Anand's invention—the zero-rupee note. Anand is a social reformer in India whose mission is to mobilize average citizens to fight corruption. In a recent effort, he designed and printed 2 million zero-rupee notes. When rolled or folded, the notes look like real currency that people can pass to officials who solicit them for bribes. When the official later opens the note in private, he instead sees an anticorruption message printed next to the face of Mohandas Gandhi.

Global Citizenship in Extractive Industries

Collective approaches are emerging in a variety of industries. The Extractive Industries Transparency Initiative (EITI) is another effort like PACI that garners the support of governments and companies to fight misallocation of funds. First initiated in 2003 by the government of U.K. Prime Minister Tony Blair and a coalition of nonprofits called Publish What You Pay, EITI signatories in the oil and gas and natural resources industries agreed to publish the terms of contract agreements between extraction firms and countries that own the natural resources. EITI attacks the problem from both sides: extraction firms publish what they pay to countries in exploration licenses or resource revenues, and the countries themselves publish what they receive. If the numbers don't match, then something has happened to the funds in between.

EITI is not perfect. Participation and disclosure are voluntary, and many companies resist the mandatory reporting requirements. Demanding virtue in business dealings can be rough as well. In 2001, BP was almost kicked out of Angola for making public its payment of a $111 million signature bonus to the government.

The benefits of taking the lead in global citizenship can accrue to companies that find themselves at the forefront of social change. Indeed, many initiatives like PACI and EITI come ahead of wider government policy. The U.S. Congress has passed a bill that would require U.S. extraction firms to publish payments to governments as part of their SEC filings. The European Commission is looking to do the same.

The advantage of programs like PACI and EITI is that they begin to address the issue of corruption by changing the calculus of whether to play along with a corrupt official. Today, when a government funds a major infrastructure project or resource exploration project and members of PACI or EITI withdraw from the process, it's a clear indication that corruption is a problem, without putting any of the members into direct conflict with government officials. There is a long way to go, but this safety-in-numbers approach will eventually make it difficult to hide corrupt practices and the Bill Browders of the world will no longer have to stand alone. As more firms sign on, the gaps in data get smaller and there are fewer places for corruption to hide.

Standards of Practice

Boeckmann and Browder are pioneers in rooting out corruption and are, without a doubt, leaders in citizenship. They recognize that their actions either affirm corrupt practice or work to change it.

There is still a long way to go. Despite encouraging examples like PACI, critics of world trade claim that globalization is nothing more than a race to the bottom between companies jockeying to establish operations in jurisdictions with lax social and environmental regulations, the lowest wages, and the weakest worker protections. During the 1990s especially, the media were filled with stories about the major brands like Gap, Levi Strauss, and Nike using sweatshop factories and child labor in countries from Honduras to Bangladesh. It seemed common practice to turn a blind eye to sweatshops in order to provide affordable products. Some influential commentators on international development policy even argue that sweatshops are better than the alternatives, since they offer formal employment in places where it is scarce.[10] Firms that acquiesce to and become complicit in corruption likewise claim that it is impossible to do business any other way. For some firms, it is easier to look for reasons to justify their actions than change their approach.

But change is happening, albeit slowly. Public pressure coupled with the leadership vision of some true global citizens has led to widespread adoption of codes of conduct in industries like textiles, electronics, and petrochemicals. These codes require participating companies to ensure that their suppliers are complying with a range of requirements for working conditions, environmental performance, and so on. Companies don't just take their suppliers' word for it. They check compliance with onsite audits and third-party verification.

The slow spread of codes of conduct has created a real-world opportunity for scholars to design experiments that evaluate whether higher wages cause job losses. Ann Harrison and Jason Scorse, academics at University of California, Berkeley, and the Monterey Institute of International Studies, respectively, conducted a study to measure the effect of wage increases on the textile, footwear, and apparel industries in Indonesia.[11] They found that the anti-sweatshop campaigns resulted in large increases in wages—sometimes doubling the workers' income—but did not affect the number of people those factories employed overall. There were costs, of course: investment in capital slowed, some smaller firms closed entirely or left the Indonesian market, and profits of the firms fell. But the idea that a race to the bottom is inevitable, that leaders have to choose between treating workers fairly and offering jobs, is wrong.

Of course, creating standards and enforcing them is not cost-free for businesses, and in an ideal world, private companies would not be solely responsible for ensuring compliance. National governments and regulations would also do their part to protect the welfare of employees and citizens. But operating globally means confronting situations where local governments are unable or unwilling to provide needed social protections. Paying a living wage costs more, but it doesn't necessarily lead to massive layoffs or capital flight to the next low-wage haven. It is best managed as an investment in the growth, prosperity, and stability of the communities in which a company is operating, one that may result in decreased business risk and enhanced local productivity.

Intel in Costa Rica: A Race to the Top in Global Citizenship

Intel's approach to expansion in Costa Rica shows how a firm can flip the equation in foreign operations from a race to the bottom to a race to the top. In the mid-1990s, Intel had plans to build a new testing and assembly facility in order to meet demand for its products. Intel already had operations in Malaysia and China, as well as in Europe and the United States. Putting the new plant in Latin America offered an opportunity to spread its international risk exposure. After considering Brazil, Mexico, and Chile, the firm ultimately decided to build its new $300 million plant in Costa Rica.

Costa Rica was not an obvious choice. The other contenders had higher populations of educated professionals, less-expensive energy costs, and existing clusters of high-tech companies. Though Costa Rica had a well-educated population and a growing economy, its GDP was dominated by coffee and banana exports, and some low-skill apparel and textile activity. But Intel executives were impressed by the Costa Rican approach. There was less talk about exclusive tax breaks and sweet deals and more conversation about how they could work together to collectively create economic and governance conditions that were favorable to Intel's and, ultimately, Costa Rica's success in the global marketplace.

Choosing Costa Rica put Intel into a pioneering position. The government would make some changes to existing policies on volume charging for energy consumption, education curricula, and airport traffic. These were all initiated to accommodate Intel's needs, but both parties agreed that Intel should not receive special treatment. Any changes in policy or law needed to be universal, so that any large firm could take advantage of them. This served Costa Rica's larger goal of promoting itself as a location for large, foreign tech and electronics firms. It also protected Intel from the possibility that a change in government might bring a less generous administration to power and put the firm's investment at risk.

During a panel discussion at Thunderbird in 2006, Craig Barrett, Intel's CEO at the time, described how the commitment of Costa Rica's president, José María Figueres, to passing stronger business regulations influenced the firm's decision to invest in Costa Rica. President Figueres reminded the audience that Intel requests were good not just for Intel, but for Costa Rica: the regulations put in place made the country more competitive. This was a case of two global leaders—one in business, one in government—demonstrating global citizenship that created shared value for all parties.

The development benefits that a country can gain from having a major multinational foreign direct investor are huge. For a country as small as Costa Rica, a firm like Intel, whose annual worldwide earnings in the mid-1990s were nearly twice the Costa Rican GDP, would create big benefits in employment, exports, tax revenues, and other benefits. In his presentation at Thunderbird, Figueres likened the impact of the Intel investment in the Costa Rican economy amounted to "replacing the engine of a Volkswagen Beetle with a jet engine from a Boeing 747." Workers' advocates may look at this willing investor and (overly) eager government and see a situation ripe for exploitation of the vulnerable. But Intel has contributed more than jobs and tax revenue to the country. In contrast to the typical narrative of low wages and poor conditions, Intel's investments in Costa Rica include significant enhancements to the country's educational system, stretching all the way from college-level course materials to the secondary grades. While generous, there was also a good deal of enlightened self-interest.

When Intel first considered Costa Rica as a location for its assembly and testing facility, the firm was legitimately concerned that the country did not have enough skilled professionals to fill the needed positions. An assembly and testing facility is not as sophisticated as a semiconductor fab, but Intel still needed eight hundred midlevel technicians to start, and fifteen hundred when the plant was fully operational. This was a large number of skilled specialists for a country with only 3.5 million citizens. For the Costa Rican negotiators, Intel's needs were in perfect alignment with the country's needs. Since the early years of the twentieth century, Costa Rica had had a history of significant investments in its primary and secondary education infrastructure, and a more recent focus on math and science had cultivated strong educational institutions that turned out skilled professionals. But Intel needed more.

In response, the firm collaborated with the Costa Rican government and two of the country's public institutions, the Technical Institute of Costa Rica and the University of Costa Rica, to enhance the existing educational programs. From 1998 to 2000, the first two years of the collaboration, Intel provided training programs to university professors to improve their skills; it donated equipment to be used for students' hands-on training and skill development; and it offered scholarships for both engineering and English as a Second Language (ESL) courses.

The success of the first effort spurred Intel. A second phase of investment began in 2000, when Intel decided to create an engineering center in Costa Rica to contribute to its worldwide initiatives around very-large-scale integrated circuits, networking, and wireless products. The three hundred–strong staff of the center would be engineers, a more highly skilled group than the technicians at the assembly and testing plant. To prepare Costa Ricans to succeed in those jobs, Intel worked again with its university partners to develop courses that would equip graduates with the computer science and electrical engineering skills they would need at Intel.

In the third phase, which began in 2002, Intel sought to expand the pool of professionals skilled in component design, package development, product development, manufacturing, software development, and research—all areas that the firm had previously concentrated in different geographies. To meet these goals, Intel again worked with the universities to fund the creation of specialized labs with specialty equipment and set up research study-abroad programs for PhD candidates.

Intel's education efforts did not stop with the universities. As soon as it arrived on Costa Rican soil, the firm began investing in the basic sciences and math programs at the country's technical high schools and worked to expand the capacity of ESL programs by training teachers and funding resources. The Intel Teach to the Future (ITTF) program for training master teachers in participatory teaching methods that employ technology has been shown to improve teacher skills and student learning. In Costa Rica, 20 percent of the country's K–12 teachers had received the training by 2004.

All of these efforts naturally serve Intel's interests at the same time that they enhance the skills and capacities of Costa Rica's institutions and the people they serve. In so many ways, investing in Costa Rica's education system is just smart business. In 2004, Intel's education budget in Costa Rica was $950,000. From 1998, when these programs began, to 2003, Intel hired only 10 percent of the graduates of the technical programs that it supported. The majority of the remaining graduates were employed by other companies in the electronics and technology sector, some of which are Intel suppliers, and all of which have contributed to growing the share of Costa Rican exports that come from the electronics sector.[12] In doing so, Intel has become a citizen, a native of Costa Rica, contributing to the country's growth and benefiting from its economic success.

Building Prosperity for All

There is a certain moral clarity to the examples of combating corruption in the examples of Fluor, PACI, and Bill Browder. Few would argue against the benefits of Intel's adherence to a higher standard of worker skill development. But it should be said that global citizenship is not always so clear. When Nike manufacturing partners in Pakistan employ eight-year-olds to make soccer balls for pennies a day, the moral imperative is clear; such practices would be unacceptable in Nike's Portland, Oregon, headquarters, so they should be unacceptable anywhere Nike flies its brand banner. But where is the cutoff? In the West, we consider people under sixteen years old to be children, but that standard does not hold around the world. And what about the worker who is of age by any standard and the income, paltry for the West, is the going wage for such work in the region?

We discussed in chapter 3 how competitiveness in an international environment partly requires the ability to identify the advantages that one geography offers over another. Recall that Apple can make the iPhone at a price that people can afford because the infrastructure and labor costs paid by Foxconn in Shenzhen keep product prices low. Why else would companies manufacture far away from their selling markets?

Economists and other observers assert that companies that bring jobs to impoverished regions are helping pave the road to prosperity through reliable employment, and that their continued presence there relies on the continued competitiveness of the region and of their spending. But is it enough to just bring jobs when there is so much greater need for employees, employees' families, and partner networks?

Companies like Intel believe it is not and see shared value in contributing to social progress. Intel is not alone; there are others with a larger idea of responsibility taking steps to fill the gaps in the communities in which they operate. Like Intel, mining giant Freeport McMoRan announced a partnership with Thunderbird in 2011 to train women entrepreneurs in mining towns in Chile and Peru, with the goal of creating a sustainable local economy that would survive the life of the mine.

Another mining company, Debswana Diamond Mining Company, a De Beer's joint venture with the South African government, identified that 35 percent of its employees in mines in South Africa were HIV positive. Beyond the tragic circumstance, having a third of the workforce infected with HIV poses obvious practical problems for the company. In the interest of keeping its employees healthy and working, the company made antiretroviral drugs available to its HIV-positive employees and their families. This effort began in 2001, before the South African government began offering treatment to people living with HIV/AIDS. By stepping into a gap in the social fabric, Debswana has benefited from a significant decline in sick leave as a result of the program.

Programs such as those offered by Debswana are possible in part as a result of citizenship work within the pharmaceutical industry. That citizenship takes one of two forms: the first is in the innovation in drugs to combat disease; and the second in making those drugs available to populations that need them at prices they can afford.

Global Citizenship in Disease Control

Dr. Joseph Kim, CEO of Inovio, is also working to make needed medications for the world's poor. As the founder of VGX Pharmaceuticals, Dr. Kim had worked on a newer class of vaccines, called DNA vaccines, to combat complex diseases such as HIV/AIDS, influenza, and various cancers. After merging VGX and Inovio Pharmaceuticals, Dr. Kim has continued that work. His company has a number of experimental HIV vaccines in human tests, as well as a universal vaccine to combat pandemic and seasonal flu.

Traditional vaccines use either a live, weakened form of a virus, or a killed virus, to train a person's immune system to deal with that virus when it confronts it in the future. Traditional vaccine technology has rid the world of smallpox; reduced the threat of former world scourges such as polio, measles, and rubella; and improved the health and quality of life for millions. Yet a number of virology experts, Kim included, believe science has reached the limits of traditional vaccine technology. Pathogens such as HIV, malaria, influenza, and tuberculosis, adapt and mutate rapidly in response to new threats. These adaptable pathogens require new methods to attack them.

Global citizenship comes into play when the need for new methods comes in conflict with pharmaceutical economics. The research and development expenses in the pharmaceutical industry are astronomical, but are worth it for the firm that discovers an effective drug for which it holds a profitable patent. Profit, by definition, comes from selling drugs to people or institutions that can pay. Yet some of the world's most widespread and deadly diseases, such as HIV/AIDS, malaria, and tuberculosis, disproportionately affect the world's poor, who often have no means to pay. What's worse is that poor children are more likely to die from these diseases, given the immaturity of their young immune systems. The developing nations of Sub-Saharan Africa, South and Central Asia, and Latin America, where these illnesses are common, likewise lack the government budgets to pay for medicines and the public health-care infrastructure to equitably distribute medicines to everyone who needs them. As a consequence, pharmaceutical companies looking for projects with high-profit potential often shy away from diseases of poverty.

Seeing both need and opportunity, Kim entered into a partnership with the Malaria Vaccines Initiative (MVI), a nonprofit funded by the Bill & Melinda Gates Foundation. MVI is funding Inovio's research and development of a vaccine to fight malaria using Inovio's synthetic DNA vaccine development technology. Inovio, in turn, is creating the vaccine compounds and seeing them through the various phases of animal and human testing to licensure. If Inovio successfully develops a malaria vaccine that protects more than 50 percent of people who receive it, then the two organizations will share the proceeds (50 percent protection is currently the best result a malaria vaccine has achieved in human trials, in this case a vaccine developed by GlaxoSmithKline [GSK] and MVI). MVI will own the distribution rights for all the countries of the developing world, and Inovio will own the distribution rights for developed countries, a market that serves Western travelers.

Kim says, "Being able to make an impact in a real scourge like malaria, especially when it gets to be so far reaching in the lives of children around the world, was a big attraction for us. In Africa and Southeast Asia, malaria is impacting the whole society. Is this something we would have been able to go after on our own? Probably not—we are still a for-profit investor entity. But I am very proud of the relationship we have developed with Gates/MVI. It is a fair partnership in which both parties can succeed."

Making Health Affordable

In addition to development, the pharmaceutical industry has also made inroads in making drugs available to needy populations. For the reasons outlined earlier, the industry has not always embraced this part of its citizenship. Innovations that lead to treatments for previously untreatable ailments and diseases come at a cost, and pharmaceutical companies have been unwilling to put in the investment to develop a drug that they have no hope of selling. This hurts everyone, especially those who need drugs the most.

A number of leaders are working to change the equation for pharmaceutical companies. Global leaders like Owen Barder, Michael Kremer, and others at the nonprofit Center for Global Development (CGD) think tank in Washington, D.C., pioneered the concept of advanced market commitments (AMC) for vaccines for neglected diseases, for instance. An AMC allows philanthropic donors and national governments to pledge guaranteed funds for purchasing a vaccine once it is developed. AMCs rely on a market test; in order to qualify to receive AMC funds, pharmaceutical companies must not only develop a vaccine but widely deploy it.

AMCs reduce risk for pharmaceutical firms because they know if they develop a product, they will earn a return on it. The approach has already led to the development and wide deployment of a new pneumococcal vaccine that has the potential to prevent illness and death for tens of thousands of the world's young children each year.

In the case of HIV/AIDS drugs, the pharmaceutical industry initially resisted the call to offer antiretroviral drugs at reduced cost to countries with a high burden of disease and little ability to pay. The concern over HIV/AIDS drugs was that lower prices for one country would result in cries for preferential pricing for other regions or groups. The concerns reached even farther: if concessions are made for one drug, why not for the rest of a pharmaceutical company's product portfolio?

This slippery slope was surmounted when Indian pharmaceutical manufacturer Cipla, with the support of the Indian government, unilaterally began producing patent-protected antiretroviral drugs, causing the economics of the drugs to implode. That move opened the way for organizations such as the Clinton Foundation and others to work with the industry to develop a tiered pricing approach for different regions. Today, companies such as Merck and GSK sell antiretroviral drugs in impoverished regions at or slightly above cost. Nonprofit and government aid organizations buy significant volumes of drugs, and the pharmaceutical companies have higher pricing models for wealthier regions where the ability to pay is higher and profits are possible.

HIV/AIDS drugs are a good example because the disease is so well known and has such high impact. Yet HIV/AIDS is by no means the only disease that has benefited from the pharmaceutical industry's citizenship. For instance, Swiss pharmaceutical company Novartis has done significant work on leprosy. Its work has aimed to reduce the stigma and promote the understanding of leprosy as a treatable infectious disease. To that end, the firm has developed radio jingles and produced a television romance that aired in Sri Lanka in which leprosy comes between two lovers— until the young man is cured. Novartis also offers drugs to combat the infectious disease and delivers them in blister packs so they stay clean, can be easily counted, and can be returned to the distributor for better inventory management. This approach helps distributors know that the drugs were used properly, according to the defined regimen.

Another example of how global citizenship has changed the industry is GSK and Merck's commitments to dramatically reduce or eliminate a number of what are known as *neglected tropical diseases* or NTDs. NTDs, such as parasitic worm infections, affect billions in developing countries but have historically received little attention from developed world pharmaceutical companies. The Abdul Latif Jameel Poverty Action Lab, a research center at MIT, has identified worms as an important cause of school absenteeism and it has calculated that deworming is one of the most cost-effective interventions to increase school participation. Both Merck and GSK had drugs (ivermectin and albendazole, respectively) that fight parasites effectively—though they were developed primarily for veterinary applications. As early as the mid-1980s limited donations of these drugs were being made to global health programs. But by the beginning of the twenty-first century, these firms had reached a new seriousness about tackling NTDs.

For instance, in a presentation to senior leadership, GSK scientists showed that if albendazole was used consistently over a five-year period in endemic countries, lymphatic filiarisis (LF, also know as elephantiasis), an NTD that causes crippling fevers and swelling of the limbs, could be eliminated from the planet. The catch? It would require a twenty-year commitment at a cost of

$1 billion to provide the treatment needed for the 1 billion infected and susceptible populations. In 2008, GSK officially began its program to rid the world of this disease. Merck and GSK have continued to up the ante, expanding their programs in the last few years to provide as much albendazole and ivermectin as necessary to not only eliminate LF but to provide deworming treatments for all school-aged children around the world in regions where parasitic worm infections are common.[13]

Reaching Sustainability

In its own way, vehicle manufacturer Toyota recognizes the responsibility of citizenship in the communities in which it operates. In one instance in the 1970s, Toyota increased its presence within Indonesia after its factories and showrooms had been damaged during the country's civil war. According to Akira Yokoi, the section manager for Toyota in Indonesia at the time, part of the company's commitment was to help Indonesia industrialize and develop demand for cars, no small feat in a place where all the bridges had been destroyed and there was almost no commercial market. In response, Toyota developed an affordable car called the Kijan that could be assembled in local factories employing local people.

Toyota's action in Indonesia is consistent with the company's philosophy that it has a commitment to the communities it serves. Yet Toyota is a manufacturing company; it never loses sight of that. As such, it seeks as much as possible to fulfill its commitment within its core function of making high-quality products that people want and can afford. The Kijan was its solution for the Indonesian market in the 1970s. Today, it fills a similar role with the Prius.

The Prius dates back to 1992, when Toyota in Japan published a document called the "Earth Charter," which communicated its intention to develop the lowest-emission cars possible. In 1992, climate change was a new international environmental issue, and public understanding of the role of human activity in environmental change was not widespread.

Nonetheless, recognizing a problem, Toyota set out to design a low-emissions vehicle. It developed a prototype by 1995, and was selling the car in Japan two years later, before any other automotive manufacturer had a competing product. At the time, Toyota was ridiculed by its peers. No one believed that the driving public would buy a gas-electric hybrid vehicle. The idea was even used as a political jab against Al Gore during the 2000 U.S. presidential campaign. And in the early years, the sales of the Prius did not prove that view wrong. Only eighteen thousand cars sold in the first year, and Toyota was pricing the Prius so low that it was literally losing money on each car sold.

Ten years later, life looked very different for the Prius. In 2008, Toyota announced that more than 1 million Prius vehicles had sold since its launch, and an entire market has developed around low-emissions vehicles. The Prius brand has become the Kleenex or Xerox of hybrid vehicles. Today, U.S. manufacturers Ford and GM seem to be building their futures on hybrid and electric technology, while Nissan has released the all-electric LEAF at a midrange price. Toyota offers an example of how an idea oriented around global citizenship—even one that seems so obvious in retrospect—could contribute to a portfolio of solutions to the seemingly intractable problem of climate change. But it required a commitment of attacking society's challenges and a long-term view.

Toyota also displayed its citizenship during the 2008 recession in the way it treated its employees. The dip in the economy corresponded with one of the greatest challenges Toyota has ever faced. In 2009 and 2010, Toyota recalled millions of vehicles in response to claims that they were accelerating uncontrollably. In one tragic case, a family died in a Lexus they had borrowed from the dealer while their own car was being serviced. That accident received a lot of coverage, as newspaper articles worldwide speculated on whether Toyota vehicles were safe to drive. An intensive investigation by the National Highway Transportation Safety Administration ultimately exonerated Toyota, but it took nearly a year to complete. Toyota vehicle sales plummeted, helped in their downward direction by the long-term declines the whole industry experienced as a result of the global recession.

During the long investigation, Toyota had a huge drop in profitability and sales from a combination of tepid market conditions, lost consumer confidence, and recall expenses. Yet, despite these challenges and financial pressures, Toyota did not engage in any involuntary layoffs. Toyota's commitment to long-term employment for its employees dates back to the 1950s when Kiichiro Toyoda was at the helm. The firm became overextended and was forced by lenders to lay off a large number of workers. Toyoda designated himself as the first employee to be laid off; the firm itself committed to a long-term strategy to never be forced by outsiders to lay off workers again. Toyota views its workers as incredibly rich sources of organizational knowledge and experience. Recessions are temporary, but a person's skills, when cultivated and maintained, are permanent. So Toyota does everything it can to keep its workers on its payrolls. It even used downtime in the plants to conduct trainings and improve processes so that the workers would be even more effective when demand rose, which it did toward the end of 2010.[14]

The Citizen Entrepreneur

One of the important elements that link Fluor, Intel, Inovio, and Toyota is the fact that these profit-making companies are all engaging in global citizenship in a way consistent with their commercial aspirations. Toyota's development of the Kijan also illustrates that the poor themselves—or the countries where they live—can be customers too.

Paul Meyer, the founder of Voxiva, is counting on it.

When Meyer graduated from Yale Law School, he refused to accept the dilemma he seemed to be presented with—either public service or profit making, in his words, to "either join the Peace Corps or McKinsey." Meyer rejected this as a false choice. He intended to be a financially successful businessperson and make the world a better place at the same time. After several initiatives and career turns, he would find a way to do just that: Voxiva.

Voxiva is a for-profit venture Meyer launched with the aim of creating a technology platform to enable unobstructed information flow between the places and individuals in the world that have problems and the places that have resources to solve them. This may seem like an obvious idea in the Internet age; there has been no shortage of ideas for linking people through the use of technology. But not all technology systems work in all contexts. Where there is no network infrastructure, no linkage to the electric grid and widespread illiteracy, Internet or wireless solutions fail.

Mobile network infrastructure is increasingly penetrating around the world, and mobile phone adoption is expanding in kind, even among the poor. Yet, as with all innovations, adoption is uneven. In Kenya, cell phone use in some rural villages is widespread. In Bolivia, it is practically nonexistent. As a result, there remain many rural communities for which the only link to the outside world for many miles is a single village phone. Voxiva's initial efforts focused on these remote regions through the systems those regions have.

Voxiva's first project involved setting up a medical reporting system in a remote region of Peru, called the Alerta system. With funding from the Markle Foundation, Ben Cohen of Ben & Jerry's fame, and the World Bank, Meyer and Voxiva launched a program to enable health workers in Peru's remote Andean villages to report health information to a central government system by using the village touch-tone phone. Village health workers were given cards with simple, picture-based instructions to navigate the system. By receiving health and disease information in this way, the Peruvian health ministry was able to identify needs that it otherwise would not have known about. Alerta even allowed the country to get notification when one village developed a few cases of Bartonellosis, a potentially fatal illness transmitted by sand flies and marked by fever and seizures. That information allowed the government to send university doctors to treat the ill and prevent a more widespread outbreak.

Since launching this proof of concept, Voxiva has developed other disease surveillance systems: it has created a program for the Peruvian navy, a system that allowed the U.S. Department of Defense to track adverse reactions to smallpox vaccination among armed forces personnel, and a telephone-based system for the U.S. Food and Drug Administration to track blood shortages among the country's blood banks. Voxiva's projects are not limited to land-based telephone systems. Recently, the firm developed a platform for managing the informative text messages developed by the U.S. Centers for Disease Control and Prevention and sent to pregnant women and new mothers on how to have a healthy pregnancy and healthy baby. These projects also show how Voxiva has moved away from nonprofit funding toward investments consistent with the firm's focus on providing its solutions on a commercial basis. Of his journey, Meyer says, "Why would I worry more about a factory worker in Michigan than a farmer in Peru? As a citizen of the world I want to make a difference in whatever way I can, to whomever can benefit the most."

Becoming a Global Citizen

Among the three pillars of effective global leadership, global citizenship may be the most difficult characteristic to teach and indeed to learn. Many aspects of global mindset can be taught, particularly when it comes to intellectual capital; likewise, entrepreneurial skills for business plan development, market analysis, and opportunity identification can be sharpened in a classroom environment.

Global citizenship is different. It is not about knowledge or skills, but about values that define how you behave in complex situations, how you resolve conflicting priorities, and how you define success. When the context is ambiguous, global citizenship equips you to make the right call in a way that fulfills the requirement of creating value for everyone affected.

For many of you, the value systems that define what you believe as right or wrong come to you from your parents or your community. They are part of who you are, not a mantle you wear. Yet circumstances can and do continue to shape your value system well into adulthood. Personal experience with poverty, disease, or injustice may alert you to issues you used to ignore. Membership in new professional communities or a training program in a new job can expand your understanding of how your actions create consequences. Organizational culture and routines can help you develop certain habits. Your interactions with others can influence and reinforce the way you see the world. The Spanish proverb, "Tell me who you hang out with and I'll tell you who you are," sums it up: global citizenship is the outcome of who you are *and* who you choose to surround yourself with.[15] Thus, the best way to develop global citizenship is to surround yourself with people who share your commitment.

As part of creating communities of people who uphold certain values, business schools play an important role, both in forming students' values and in influencing the downstream cultures of the firms those students later come to lead. During the global financial crisis of 2007–2009—which is still reverberating through much of the world—there was criticism from many sides about the value systems that business schools are indoctrinating into their students. These concerns, unfortunately, are well founded. Data from the Aspen Institute shows that in the two years that students spend earning their MBAs, their opinions change about what business leaders should prioritize: graduating students are much more likely than incoming students to name shareholder value maximization as the top priority for a business leader. Academic experiences for these individuals are hugely influential and leave indelible marks on their value systems.

Some pundits and academics question whether graduate schools should be attempting to alter the values of future managers. These questions ignore the reality that education institutions already do that, and not necessarily consciously or in the right direction. If business schools—and the employers that recruit from them—want to have a positive influence on the value systems of aspiring leaders, they need to walk the walk. They need to have a set of positive, society-oriented values incorporated into their cultures and reflected in their ways of speaking, practices, and rewards systems. Students—and the employees they become—in turn need to choose the institutions and organizations that act in ways that correspond with their beliefs.

One concrete effort to bring values to the fore in management education has been spearheaded by the dominant trade associations in Europe, the European Foundation for Management Development (EFMD), and in the United States, the Association to Advance Collegiate Schools of Business (AACSB), in partnership with the United Nations and other multilateral and nongovernmental organizations. These organizations have launched an initiative, Principles for Responsible Management Education. These six principles, in whose gestation we were both involved, offer a voluntary set of guidelines that business schools can follow to promote ideas of sustainability and responsibility in their developing leaders.[16] So far over three hundred business schools around the world have endorsed the principles.[17]

Practicing Citizenship: The Thunderbird Oath of Honor and the Oath Project

Thunderbird has long identified global citizenship as one of its core values. The campus's main gate greets departing visitors with Socrates' statement, "I am not an Athenian or a Greek, but a citizen of the world." We see management as a true, honorable profession, and we believe we have a responsibility to give our graduates not only the tools of leadership, but also guidance on how to use those tools in ethical ways that create what our mission statement refers to as "sustainable prosperity worldwide." One way that we ingrain these values in our faculty, staff, and educational and corporate activities was inspired by another great Greek, Hippocrates.

When Hippocrates first began teaching medicine in the fourth century BC, he recognized his students could use their skills to both save lives and extinguish them. Ever since, the Hippocratic Oath admonition to "do no harm" has been core to medical school teaching. In 2005, the Thunderbird community developed and adopted an Oath of Professional Honor, perhaps the first of its kind for a business school, which is now recited by all graduating students during commencement:

As a Thunderbird and a global citizen, I promise:
I will strive to act with honesty and integrity,
I will respect the rights and dignity of all people,
I will strive to create sustainable prosperity worldwide,
I will oppose all forms of corruption and exploitation, and
I will take responsibility for my actions.
As I hold true to these principles, it is my hope that I may enjoy an
    honorable reputation and peace of conscience.
This pledge I make freely and upon my honor.

The oath has inspired both admiration and criticism. One of the most cited concerns is that it is too naive and that it has "no teeth." As a voluntary, unenforceable code, there is obviously the risk that graduates will sign it, but go on to behave in any way they wish. That criticism misses the point. The oath is not simply a nice exercise in ritual. It is a defining document, a set of core values and commitments that fully define Thunderbird's academic and social culture. It is at once a product of those values and a tool to reinforce them. The school's experience offers a case study in what an organizational culture can instill in its community members. Our students, colleagues, alumni, trustees, and other members of our community are constantly pushing us to live up to the intention of the oath. The school's explicit commitment to those values has encouraged countless initiatives, curricular changes, and voluntary programs on campus.

For example, student teams set out to help the school understand its environmental footprint and discover ways to improve it. The student-led Thunderbird Climate Initiative began as a project in the traditional business intelligence course as an effort to map our sources of carbon emissions. The teams then went on to implement projects to reduce our climate impact through awareness campaigns and energy-efficiency improvement efforts.

The commitment to the oath has also raised the expectations of our applicants, students, donors, and broader community, and has created real social costs for anyone who acts inconsistently with the oath. That academic culture is the best tool at our disposal, perhaps the only tool, to have a positive impact on the value systems of the thousands of students and executives who populate our classrooms every year.

The contributions of our students are not in any way trivial. The global leaders we've profiled in this chapter are often in a position—as a function of their leadership roles—to create change. But the decisions and actions made on the ground by the thousands of employees at those leaders' firms offer the true measure of a firm's citizenship, just as the actions of our graduates after they leave Thunderbird are the strongest measures of the school's commitment to citizenship. Babson College Professor Mary Gentile has powerfully argued that cultures of responsibility are only possible when every individual in an organization can have the courage to speak up for what he or she thinks is right; Gentile has developed an entire curriculum, "Giving Voice to Values," to empower employees and managers to act on their values despite opposing pressures from others.[18]

The Thunderbird oath serves as a way for us to empower every individual to commit and stand up for his or her values in global citizenship. We hope to both influence everyone we come in contact with and attract those who aspire to live with integrity. For that reason, the school first asks applicants to read and respond to the oath during the application process; this sends a clear signal to potential candidates that joining Thunderbird means you are joining a community that shares values and expectations about your professional behavior.

The idea that values should shape business dealings has gained significant traction in the years since Thunderbird developed its oath. Harvard Business School dean Nitin Nohria and Harvard professor Rakesh Khurana argued in a 2008 article in the *Harvard Business Review* that management ought to be treated as a true profession, rooted not only in solid knowledge and skills but also in a code of professional conduct.[19] World Economic Forum founder and chairman Klaus Schwab made similar arguments in a 2009 *New York Times* op-ed that laid out his six objectives for that year's meeting in Davos. Number four was "to improve the ethical base for business as a constructive social actor."[20]

Schwab's vision has not fallen flat. The World Economic Forum's Young Global Leaders produced the Global Business Oath in 2009. In that same year, a group of Harvard MBA students convinced over half of their graduating class to sign an oath that later became known as the MBA Oath, now with chapters in dozens of other business schools. These various efforts converged in a new initiative, the Oath Project, an effort to spreading the values of global citizenship through business schools and corporations.[21] The UN, World Economic Forum, Aspen Institute, and other influential organizations support the Oath Project's mission to inspire individuals to the high standards of management as a profession.

Practicing Citizenship: Thunderbird for Good

The oath is an important part of Thunderbird's efforts to fulfill its commitment to educate global leaders who create sustainable prosperity worldwide. For many years, Thunderbird interpreted that commitment exclusively by educating the students who enrolled in the school so they could best fulfill their roles as global leaders. More recently, however, the two of us and many of our colleagues have started to think more deeply about the meaning of the mission. Global leaders operate around the world, and each aspires to make a difference to their communities, whether those communities are entire countries or small villages, affluent or struggling. Yet very few global entrepreneurs are in the financial position to take advantage of a Thunderbird education. Given the school's mission of educating global leaders who create sustainable prosperity worldwide, shouldn't global citizenship at Thunderbird involve doing what we can to make that education available to people who otherwise could not access it?

The school had just begun considering ways to act on that intent when Barbara Barrett, a Thunderbird trustee in 2004, challenged the school to come up with a plan to educate Afghanistan's aspiring women entrepreneurs. As we described in chapter 2, Barrett possesses an extraordinary amount of global social capital and, with it, an ability to be very convincing. She had been very active in Afghanistan's women's groups, had made several trips to the country, and wanted Thunderbird to bring its expertise to help the war-torn country in its development.

From that initial challenge, Thunderbird developed Project Artemis, an intensive entrepreneurial training program. Fifteen Afghan women came to Thunderbird for two weeks in 2005 to learn strategy, business plan development, marketing, accounting, finance, and other core skills from Thunderbird faculty. The Project Artemis women networked with Thunderbird students, alumni, and other community members. All were given computers and matched with personal mentors to advise and guide them as they developed their businesses. One Project Artemis alumna is Rangina Hamidi, a global entrepreneur we profiled in chapter 3.

Thunderbird originally created Project Artemis because the school was motivated to expand its mission to nontraditional students, and Barrett gave a focus for doing it. We knew from the outset that the training and networking needed to make a difference in the lives of the student-entrepreneurs. The income of those businesses can be huge. Former students say that the extra money allows them to make different choices for their children. Daughters have the chance to finish school or delay marriage.

We didn't expect, however, that Project Artemis would make a difference to Thunderbird. "We really underestimated the transformational effect that the program would have on us," says Kellie Kreiser, executive director of Thunderbird for Good, the philanthropic arm of Thunderbird, formed by Ángel in the months after the first Project Artemis group came to Glendale. "That first Project Artemis had real impact on who we are and how we view ourselves. Alumni were excited; students were excited; faculty members were energized by the opportunity."

Thunderbird for Good officially formed after the first Project Artemis class graduated in 2005. Thunderbird for Good today organizes and develops all of Thunderbird's philanthropic activities, including Project Artemis and other social programs. Project Artemis continues to grow and thrive. Since graduating its first class in 2005, Project Artemis has trained four cohorts from Afghanistan totaling sixty-three students. We have also extended the project to other countries, including Jordan and Pakistan.

Over time, our intensive curriculum has evolved to keep up with the needs and existing abilities of the women who matriculate in Project Artemis and other training programs that have evolved since we started. Those abilities change all the time and vary by country. For instance, few women in the 2005 class of Afghan students knew how to turn on their computers; in the spring of 2011, a cohort from Pakistan built a Facebook page within two days of their arrival (see Project Artemis—Pakistan).[22]

As Thunderbird for Good has evolved, we've also expanded to conduct programs in developing countries with a variety of partners. We have partnered with Goldman Sachs's 10,000 Women initiative, the investment bank's philanthropic effort to provide entrepreneurial training to women in developing countries. Thunderbird has delivered the educational component for one 10,000 Women project in Afghanistan and another in Peru, which was formed under Thunderbird's Strengthening Women Entrepreneurship in Peru (SWEP) program. SWEP is an effort to improve business education and access to capital for Peruvian women entrepreneurs, cosupported by the Inter-American Development Bank.

Beyond these resource-intensive programs, Thunderbird for Good also provides opportunities for our students, alumni, staff, faculty, and any member of the broader community to contribute their skills to help someone. Our students have provided strategic planning for nonprofit groups, have created logistics plans for health program delivery in developing countries, and have partnered with their professors on long-term engagements in the social sector. These efforts are much more opportunistic than the planning-intensive nature of Project Artemis, but they do a lot to encourage the practice of global citizenship and provide skills to organizations that need them. The power of these initiatives in nurturing the values of global citizenship at Thunderbird cannot be overstated. It can serve as a reminder of how carefully crafted social engagement programs can help organizations of all kinds strengthen the commitment of its people to professional ethics and responsibility.

Global Citizenship Tools: Questions to Ask, Steps to Take

As with the other two global leadership characteristics, the first step in developing your global citizenship is to diagnose where you are now. Next, we offer some questions you can ask yourself for insight into how to think about issues of global citizenship today and provide some ideas for actions to take. To recap, global citizenship is a sensitivity to the world in which you live and your impact on it. It is also about an intention to serve the larger community and contribute to collective prosperity. As social animals, most of us are already sensitive to our context and work to fit in. The goal is to be more conscious of this natural tendency and enhance it. For more advice, see also the appendix.

Question: Do you know the names and missions of the local community groups and service organizations where you live, work, or operate?

Action: Join a group or attend some local community meetings to inform yourself of local concerns and issues, and to connect with other active citizens. Ask questions about community needs. What are the major social issues in the area? What impacts, positive and negative, do businesses in the community have on local prosperity, health, well-being, and so on?

Question: Are you informed about the political issues, parties, and candidates in the communities and regions in which you live and operate? Does your organization contribute to campaigns or lobby political officials in any areas relevant to the business? Are these political activities transparent and does the firm act with integrity in its political arrangements?

Action: If your firm has not been transparent about its interactions with public figures, ask why. Was it carelessness, oversight, or lack of internal policy? What would it take to make those activities transparent? How would you plan your strategy for political engagement if you were starting it today?

Question: Have you developed a network of community contacts? Do you know the names and positions of key stakeholders, community leaders, and opinion makers? Do you know what expectations they might have of you?

Action: Make a list of key figures in your community— from the local mayor to the volunteer head of the local youth organization. Start creating social connections with them. Seek them out at community meetings, for example, or invite them for coffee. Ask questions and listen to understand their views.

Question: Do you know what ecological region or biome you live and operate in? Is it tropical rainforest, savanna, alpine, or other? Do you know what the local resource issues are for water supply, reliable energy, safe food, and so on? Are you familiar with the local species? How dependent is the local economy on local natural resources?

Action: Connect with and support local environmental groups, universities, or zoos to familiarize yourself with the ecology of your community and build your sensitivity and awareness. The goal is not to become a PhD biologist, but to enhance your enjoyment of nature and improve your understanding of important local environmental issues so that you automatically consider them in your business dealings.

Being Global:
A Beginning

At the end of the Revolutionary War, America's founding fathers gathered in the Constitutional Convention of 1787 to hash out the political future of the new nation. Would the old-world tradition of divine right prevail? Would George Washington be crowned king? Or would a modern representative democracy emerge? Would America be the first democratic republic in centuries? Among the crowd awaiting the answer was Dr. James McHenry of Maryland. As the delegates emerged from their Independence Hall deliberations, McHenry cornered an exhausted Benjamin Franklin and asked him, "Well, Doctor Franklin, what have we got—a Republic or a Monarchy?" Franklin responded with now immortal words, "You have a republic . . . if you can keep it."

So far, the citizens of the United States have done a good job keeping their republic, but Franklin's challenge is still valid. The undertaking today, however, is not confined to any single country. It is a challenge facing everyone on the planet.

Those of us now living have received a priceless bequest from our predecessors: *a global world founded on a global marketplace.* This new world offers tremendous opportunity for shared prosperity, but it is not predestined or preordained. As recent events prove, ongoing success is uncertain, even fragile. Continuation depends on the actions of people today. We have been given a global world. Can we keep it?

By today's standards, the world of Franklin's time was a pretty miserable place. The vast majority lived on today's equivalent of $2 a day. Fortunately, there was no need to worry about retirement savings because life expectancy was only around thirty years. By the end of World War II, however, most of Western Europe, the United States, and Canada had incomes between six and ten times higher and life spans twenty-five to thirty years longer. This was driven by dramatic productivity improvements enabled by the scientific and engineering advancements of modern industrialization. In the twenty-first century, globalization continues to spread these benefits to Asia, Latin America, and the Middle East. Worldwide, the average person enjoys a life expectancy of sixty-nine years and an income of closer to $24 a day. This unprecedented transformation would have simply been impossible had the world not developed the technological tools and social institutions needed to collaborate globally through commerce.

Globalization has brought benefits to many, but not to all. International commerce has excluded many and raised questions about environmental sustainability. About 1 billion people today are hungry and trapped in extreme poverty. Education and health conditions in lower-income countries continue to be dismal compared with the developed world. These problems are not insurmountable—they can be resolved by the types of global leadership documented in this book and doing so will go a long way toward keeping and enhancing the global world we have been given. Failures of global leadership, on the other hand, could allow our global inheritance to slip away.

No political, economic, or social system is intrinsically dominant. There is no end of history. Instead, history is a constant narrative of one form of social organization overthrowing another. Regardless of the firm belief by many in the rightness of a global free and fair market, and even with the extensive proof of its social benefits, its success is not preordained.

Social order and political systems persist because people accept them. The way they are legitimized is easy to understand. The public gives power to a ruler or institution in exchange for services. As long as the public's expectations about services are fulfilled, the government is legitimate. But if the social system fails to provide the expected services, society reserves the right to "throw the bums out" and establish a new order, as Zine El Abidine Ben Ali, Muammar Gaddafi, and Hosni Mubarak learned the hard way in 2011. But it isn't just dictators and despots who are at risk. Benjamin Friedman has documented how economic struggles have reversed not just gains in financial living standards but in social inclusion, fairness, and equity throughout the United States' history.[1]

The global economic crisis we are living through as we finish this book is an example of the risks that failed global leadership portends. The financial disruption caused by the mania of short-termism and the ample examples of gains being privatized while losses are socialized has undermined faith, not just in business, but in the entire enterprise of globalization. A 2008 BBC poll found that only 5 percent of the global public believes that the economic benefits and burdens of globalization are being shared "very fairly."[2] Rampant income inequality and unemployment has sent hundreds of thousands of "indignados" to demonstrate in city squares from Athens to Madrid to New York City. In the United States, polls show that the number of people with a favorable view of the Occupy Wall Street movement vastly outnumbers those with a favorable view of the U.S. Congress.[3] There is a message here. We are in this current situation not by accident, but by decisions made by leaders in the public and private sectors. If leaders continue to act this way, they risk the future of globalization.

Today's circumstances have been hard-earned. It was built on the back of disastrous global confrontations and on the vision of global leaders who were willing to take risks to demonstrate the advantages of collaborating in pursuit of shared gains instead of isolating in hopes of private benefit. From the rubble of World War II, leaders like Jean Monnet and Robert Schuman imagined a different Europe and planted the seeds of today's European Union, which has yielded the most peaceful and prosperous decades in the continent's history. From the economic disaster of China's Great Leap Forward and Cultural Revolution, Den Xiaoping imagined a modern China engaged economically with the rest of the world. In a move that would have been unimaginable just a decade earlier, on December 11, 2001, China became a member of the World Trade Organization.

But at the end of 2011 there are plenty of dark clouds—by the time this book is published some of the hard-won gains of the last few decades may have collapsed: the European monetary union is under threat; global trade talks are all but dead and progress on joint action on climate change is exceedingly slow; several U.S. states have adopted harsh anti-immigrant policies and more are considering such measures; calls for punitive action against Chinese trade policies are growing louder.

The globalization of the world economy has proven that it *can* bring about shared prosperity, not that it necessarily *will*. For the world to reap the potential benefits of an interconnected economy, we need a corps of new leaders who have the capacity, values, and motivation to engage across cultural boundaries and find new, responsible ways to create shared value.

Throughout this book, we've called those individuals *global leaders* and have defined what they have in common and how they can be developed. Global leaders use their global mindset to connect with others, their global entrepreneurship to create value, and their global citizenship to contribute to a fairer, safer, more prosperous world. Global leaders who can effectively connect, create, and contribute are needed to reap the benefits of globalization and to demonstrate how it can bring about prosperity. Our emphasis on global citizenship as an integral part of being global is not gratuitous. It is essential both to seize the opportunity of a global economy and to ensure that the global economy does not regress into isolation.

Leaders Make a Difference

Leadership makes a difference. Business leaders and their actions have a huge impact on a firm's ability to make products and turn a profit. The effect is not trivial: the world's best-run companies are as much as 100 percent more productive than the worst-run, meaning that the best-run firms can produce twice as much value as their worst-run competitors using the same inputs.[4] Economist Nicholas Bloom at Stanford University has been leading a global research project that for the first time quantifies the impact of differences in the quality of business leadership in different countries.

His research suggests that the gap in living standards between countries can be narrowed by improving the quality of leadership and management of firms in poorer countries. In other words, quality business leadership is a technology that has not spread far and wide enough as yet.[5] Such differences matter immensely in a number of ways: highly productive firms use fewer resources to produce value, provide more stable employment, and bring prosperity to their communities. While there is less research on the impact of leaders in government or in nonprofits, there is no reason to believe that leaders have less influence on such organizations.

Global leaders yield all these benefits on a global scale. As a global leader, your impact is multiplied in the profits you earn, the jobs you produce, and the prosperity you create. *Your work matters.*

The world desperately needs global leaders to capitalize on opportunities by creating, running, or contributing to firms that join the ranks of the best run, and to lift up those in need of improvement—to solve global challenges. Some of you are profiled in this book; still others are just beginning to build your skills by developing your mindset, creating new forms of value by your entrepreneurship, and behaving with integrity and a belief that your actions should benefit all participants.

Global leaders can be made. Global leadership is a muscle that can be trained and get stronger and more dexterous with focused use and practice. Unlike muscles, however, there is no real limit to how strong you can get in your global leadership so long as you keep recommitting to your own development. The opposite, sadly, is also true. Muscles do not stay strong by themselves. Stop training and you lose strength: your intellectual capital becomes obsolete, your global connections weaken, your enterprising spirit wanes, your commitment to global prosperity fades.

Conclusion

We would like to say that momentum will keep you going and that all you need to do is start. The reality, however, is that every global leader comes to the point in his or her development when the impulse to stop training is very high. You might get bored or tired. You might get to a time in your career when you think you don't need to be as diligent anymore, that you know all you need to learn. You might have held numerous overseas posts and feel confident in your cultural agnosticism. You may feel, to extend the metaphor, you have enough muscle memory to simply coast.

We urge you not to succumb to this impulse. We urge you to recognize that once you've developed some experience in global leadership, you are at your most vulnerable. As the old adage goes, power corrupts. Recent experiments in psychology have mapped the ways in which leaders, as they climb the ladder, can become more self-centered, even justifying their own ethical lapses. In one study, behavioral psychologists at Tilberg University in the Netherlands and Northwestern University in Chicago found that people in a position of power are more likely to cheat while playing a game. Those same powerful individuals also suggested harsher punishments for cheaters who were caught.[6]

Corruption of reason occurs even in the people charged with upholding justice. A study of decisions handed down by the United States Supreme Court showed that as judges gain more power on the court, their majority opinions become less nuanced and they consider fewer alternative views. The same effect occurs when a justice becomes one of the majority party on the court.[7]

These examples may seem relatively esoteric, but they represent a systemic problem that anyone who reaches the top tier of his or her profession will face. We have all heard about, or even witnessed, situations in which respected people in positions of power engaged in immoral or illegal acts. In general, society takes a certain comfort in believing that these people are just inherently corrupt, but reality is much more nuanced. Most of the protagonists in today's cautionary tales began their careers like you and me, intending to do the right thing. They wanted to create value and make the world a better place. But somehow they lost their moorings on the way to the executive suite and the good intentions got lost.

Every leader—whether very advanced or just starting—has to guard against falling short of his or her ideals. It's the paradox of leadership: as you gain the power and experience to accomplish your goals, the subtle, often unrecognized, temptations to rely on known, familiar, and clearly controllable factors become stronger. We slip into routines and patterns. We lose energy when confronted with obstacles or entrenched ways of doing things. We resort to old modes of thinking and mental shortcuts and stop working to expand our global mindset; we pursue the same strategies with the same resources and stop looking for new sources of valuable entrepreneurship; we justify small bribes or exchanges of favor and stop upholding the ideals of citizenship. We cease being global. We cease contributing to sustainable solutions to the challenges our world faces.

The danger to all leaders is that they will become comfortable in their practices. It's entirely possible that a once-cultivated global mind will begin relying on stereotypes and simplifications. A disciplined global entrepreneur can get caught in a bureaucratic and stultifying cycle. The most committed global citizen may misstep.

Being a global leader is not a position anyone ever arrives at. It is a lifelong effort. No matter where you are in your development of a global mindset, there will be more to learn. No matter how many entrepreneurial ideas you've incubated or grown, there will be new and different sources of value to tap to create new value tomorrow. There will always be new opportunities to build an equitable and fair society, to become more sustainable, to invest in the long-term future of mutual prosperity, and to consider the question, "Are we doing the best we can?" The very characteristics of global mindset, global entrepreneurship, and global citizenship offer an antidote to power's naturally corrupting influence. These characteristics work to help leaders maintain and grow because they are not about knowledge, but about practice. They require constant reinforcement.

What can you do to ensure you continue to stretch your global mindset, that your ability to find and create new value remains nimble, and that you continue to value the contributions and protect the interests of those around you?

The first step is to recognize that your learning never ends. The second, to proactively identify and plan learning experiences to keep pushing yourself further. To grow your global mindset, you need to purposefully seek out opportunities to interact with individuals who are different from you, to become a forager for new knowledge and insights about cultures and events around the world, to put yourself in situations where you can form new relationships with individuals from around the world. Choosing what conferences to attend, what training programs to engage in, what to read and watch, and what activities to include on your next business trip are essential to your global leadership development.

To strengthen your global entrepreneurship, you need to put yourself in positions that allow you to apply your global mindset to create value. You can seek out opportunities within your organization that require you to innovate products or processes, or to expand markets, by interacting with divisions, suppliers, or clients from other countries and cultures. And you must continue to learn about key business trends in your industry beyond the market you currently serve.

And to grow as a global citizen, you must constantly renew your commitment to making a difference by surrounding yourself with individuals who can support you and strengthen your resolve. A simple beginning could be to join groups within your organization or region that are committed to expanding opportunity and holding all organizations to a high standard of accountability, to encourage your organization to join global platforms of social responsibility such as the UN Global Compact, or, at a personal level, something like the Oath Project discussed in chapter 4. Such an oath can serve as a kind of self-governance in the same way that corporate governance policies can keep the actions of the CEO in line with the firm's cultural values. The oath becomes more valuable when you make it a public commitment. The public aspect is important. Human beings are often very good at making personal commitments that come due sometime in the future ("I'm going to lose ten pounds by the holidays!") and then delaying the work required to make that commitment a reality ("I'll start tomorrow"). Most of us do better with an audience—an individual or group of people who can help us stay on track. Think of them as your personal governance board. They might be people you respect or admire, to whom you would be embarrassed to admit failure, or even who you compete with. Anyone, in short, who can remind you of your commitments and good intentions and hold you to your oath of honor.

Another benefit of the public oath is that it gives you travel companions. Find a group of like-minded friends and colleagues and make commitments together. Take one of the oaths or write a new version together that captures your personal goals for continually developing a global mindset, engaging in global entrepreneurship, and acting as a global citizen. Then make a plan to hold each other accountable to these goals.

"We Are the Ones We Have Been Waiting For"

One of Barack Obama's galvanizing slogans during his campaign for the U.S. presidency in 2008 was a call to action: "We are the ones we have been waiting for." Regardless of your personal politics, it is a helpful reminder that change is made by those who take action. It is not enough to lament the failures of current leaders or to wait for better leaders to emerge. If you want to build a more sustainable and inclusive world economy, then it is your task to become a leader who makes it happen.

The hopeful message of our book is that global leaders are not born but made. While some may be better positioned than others because of genetic fortune or family upbringing, the majority of global leaders we have studied grew into global leaders through a combination of life accidents and purposeful self-development. Our own life stories are journeys of learning to be global.

The world needs global leaders now. We hope we've inspired you to start on the path to becoming one. And we hope you'll make the lifetime commitment to pushing yourself to acquire, develop, hone, and expand the skills of a global leader. It's the only thing that will address our global challenges in a way that builds sustainable prosperity for everyone. There has never been a more opportune, or important, time for being global.

Crowdsourced Wisdom on Becoming a Global Leader

On November 10 and 11, 2011, Thunderbird hosted a Global Business Dialogue focused on issues of global leadership. During the event, we listened to, interviewed, and surveyed more than seventy-five global leaders from diverse backgrounds, industries, countries, and contexts about how global leadership is changing and what steps aspiring global leaders should take to develop their skills.

You can see video clips from many of these interviews at http://bit.ly/gbdinterviews. Here, we've summarized their input.

Global Mindset

Global mindset was the leadership capability that interviewees overwhelmingly chose as the trait most lacking in leaders today and as the trait which aspiring leaders need the most help in developing. They also clearly agreed that there is no shortcut to developing a global mindset, which perhaps explains their diagnosis of the trait as the area where existing and aspiring leaders need the most work.

So what advice did they have for improving your global mindset? Go, and stay. There was broad agreement that a global mindset has to be developed by going outside your geographic and cultural comfort zone. There is no way to learn a different perspective from afar. But the interviewees also cautioned that simply going is not enough. They noted that a global mindset requires staying outside your comfort zone for long enough to truly grasp other worldviews and perspectives. Developing a global mindset isn't measured in hours and days spent in foreign cities, but in months and years.

Another point of agreement was that becoming truly fluent in a second or third language is an invaluable way not just of expanding your ability to communicate with others but of changing the way you think. A true immersion in the idioms, jokes, and proverbs of another language will inevitably affect your perspective on the world. One interviewee suggested not only learning a foreign language but deeply studying a faith or philosophical tradition different from your own, again pointing out that this will change your perception of the world and of others.

The global leaders recommended the following books:

The Opposable Mind by Roger Martin (Boston: Harvard Business Review Press, 2007).

The Geography of Thought by Richard Nisbett (New York: Free Press, 2003).

Poor Economics by Abhijit Banerjee and Esther Duflo (New York: Public Affairs, 2011).

For everyday reading, set your Web home page to the paper of record for a country that is not your native country. One interviewee had perhaps the most dynamic suggestion regarding reading: look at *Foreign Policy*'s annual list of Global Thinkers and read their books, blogs, and tweets (see, for example, http://www.foreignpolicy.com/articles/2011/11/28/the_fp_top_100_global_thinkers).

Global Entrepreneurship

Our interviewees believed that developing global entrepreneurship, like global mindset, is primarily a hands-on activity. Many suggested actively seeking roles in start-up firms simply to gain the experience of an entrepreneurial perspective of the world. Several also emphasized the vital role of making mistakes in developing entrepreneurial skills; they believe that you learn less from studying successes than from participating in failures.

The most common advice was to find entrepreneurial mentors. Some suggested joining local, national, or international entrepreneurship organizations such as TiE (www.tie.org) or participating in the many events around the world each year as part of Global Entrepreneurship Week. Others suggested developing personal mentorship relationships, seeking out entrepreneurs you personally admire and recruiting them into your network of advisers.

One leader had advice that combined the development of a global mindset and global entrepreneurship. She suggested working for small businesses in other countries because nothing will sharpen your creative business skills and change your global perspective more than the daily battle for survival that many small businesses wage.

Global Citizenship

The leaders we interviewed generally agreed that the foundation of global citizenship is global mindset; thus there was a lot of overlap in terms of advice in these two areas. Beyond the emphasis on becoming deeply familiar with other cultures, countries, and contexts, the leaders suggested some specific steps:

- Become a regular, analytical reader of corporate social responsibility reports, studying both what organizations are doing and what they could be doing better.

- Become deeply involved in a social service organization either directly by working there or as a regular volunteer.

- Join one of the many organizations that promote workplace diversity and specifically seek out connections with people who have faced and overcome significant barriers to success. Then learn about those barriers and think about how they can be systematically eroded or removed.

- Every year, make sure you have taken an active role (not just giving to charity) in making someone else's life materially better, in a circumstance where you will receive no direct benefit. Serving the needs of one person will make you much more attuned to the needs of many others.

Role Models

Finally, we asked the interviewees to give a current example of a global leader. We were relieved to hear that Richard Branson and the Dalai Lama leaped to the minds of many leaders. The others they named are worthy role models to keep an eye on and learn from:

- Bill Gates

- Bill Clinton

- Nelson Mandela

- Indra Nooyi, chairman and CEO, PepsiCo

- Carlos Ghosn, chairman and CEO, Renault and Nissan

- Craig Barrett, former chairman and CEO, Intel

- José María Figueres, former president of Costa Rica

- Bob Dudley, group chief executive, BP

- Larry Page, cofounder, Google

NOTES

Introduction

1. Though these thought leaders and others publish in many forms, from blogs to articles, the most relevant books include: Noel Tichy and Warren Bennis, *Judgment: How Winning Leaders Make Great Calls* (New York: Portfolio, 2009); Rosabeth Moss Kanter, *SuperCorp: How Vanguard Companies Create Innovation, Profits, Growth and Social Good* (New York: Crown, 2009); John Kotter, *What Leaders Really Do* (Boston: Harvard Business School Press, 1999).

2. Unless otherwise noted, all direct quotes from these leaders are from interviews with the authors, either in person or via telephone, during the preparation of this book, 2009 to 2011.

Chapter 1

1. *New York Times* columnist Thomas Friedman argues in his book *The World Is Flat* (New York: Farrer, Strauss and Giroux, 2005) that ubiquitous communications and cross-border connectivity are allowing the world to become flat, a metaphor for frictionless connection and trade across geographies. Friedman's view is compelling, as is the counterargument proposed by Richard Florida ("The World is Spiky," *Atlantic Monthly*, October 2005, 48–51). Florida agrees that trade has changed, but he disagrees with Friedman on the point that trade is now more egalitarian as a result of global changes. Instead, Florida shows that trade concentrates in pockets (or spikes) around the globe, and that the majority of trade is not evenly distributed but highly concentrated between trading partners. The relevance of this exchange for our purposes is that the asymmetric and complex nature of trade makes country-specific understanding more important, not less, when engaging with foreign trade partners.

2. The open source project Sourcemap has documented global supply chains to create fantastical maps for items from the commonplace, such as an IKEA bed, to the celebrated, such as the Tesla Roadster. See more at http://www.sourcemap.org/.

3. W. J. Bernstein, *A Splendid Exchange: How Trade Shaped the World* (Washington, DC: Atlantic Monthly Press, 2008).

4. It has required hundreds of years of exploration and innovation to create the global connections that dominate our world today. Christopher Columbus's trans-Atlantic voyage in 1492 showed the world that the earth was not flat. The first modern international corporation emerged in the form of the Dutch East India Company, established in 1602. International travel received the additional boost in access and affordability offered by Boeing's 747, first built in 1970. The world's first direct person-to-person communications infrastructure came when the first submarine transoceanic cables were laid at the end of the nineteenth century, and continue to improve in our Internet-mobile era. Global political innovations have done their part as well, starting with the 1944 creation of an international monetary system at Bretton Woods, the 1947 GATT agreement on tariffs and trade, the period of relative post-World War II stability, and the successful creation of free-trade blocs (e.g., the European Union). These technological advances and events collectively lowered transaction costs and smoothed the flow of information to allow global engagement.

5. Data on cross-border mergers and acquisitions from United Nations Conference on Trade and Development, *2007 World Investment Report*.

6. Data on foreign direct investment from United Nations Conference on Trade and Development, *2010 World Investment Report*.

7. Data on cross-border employment from United Nations Conference on Trade and Development, *2007 World Investment Report*.

8. Ibid.

9. Relevant works by these authors include: Friedman, *The World Is Flat*; Richard Florida, *The Rise of the Creative Class* (New York: Basic Books, 2002), and "The World Is Spiky"; Robert Kagan, *The Return of History and the End of Dreams* (New York: Knopf, 2008); Jagdish Bhagwati, *In Defense of Globalization* (New York: Oxford University Press, 2004); Joseph Stiglitz, *Globalization and Its Discontents* (New York: W.W. Norton & Co., 2002); and Pankaj Ghemawat, *World 3.0: Global Prosperity and How to Achieve It* (Boston: Harvard Business Press, 2011).

10. Michael Porter and Mark Kramer, "Creating Shared Value," *Harvard Business Review*, January 2011.

11. The eight Millennium Development Goals were set in 2000 by the 189 members of the United Nations. The goals include: an end to poverty and hunger; universal access to education for all children; gender equality; child health; maternal health; combat HIV/AIDS; environmental sustainability; and develop a global partnership between nations for ongoing development. For more information, see: http://www.un.org/millenniumgoals/.

12. For more on the Global Education Initiative, see http://www.weforum.org/issues/education.

13. The terms *bridgers* and *boundary spanners* refer to individuals who are able to translate key understanding and innovation from remote corporate satellites to other locations within the firm. Bridgers in particular are those able to bring insights from developing countries back to a developed world headquarters. Thunderbird scholars Nathan Washburn and Tom Hunsaker coined the term *bridgers* in "Finding Great Ideas in Emerging Markets: Why Your Managers Need to Double as Idea Scouts," *Harvard Business Review*, September 2011, http://hbr.org/2011/09/finding-great-ideas-in-emerging-markets/ar/1. Thunderbird scholar Andreas Schötter discusses boundary spanners in his work on international development; see Andreas Schötter, "Intra-Organizational Knowledge Exchange: An Examination of Reverse-Capability Transfer in Multinational Corporations," *Journal of Intellectual Capital* 10, no. 1 (2009): 149–164.

14. S. J. Palmisano, "The Globally Integrated Enterprise," *Foreign Affairs*, May–June 2006.

Chapter 2

1. Mary Teagarden, "Learning from Toys: Reflections on the 2007 Recall Crisis," *Thunderbird International Business Review* 51, no. 1 (January–February 2009): 5–17.

2. Quote from comments made in a published exchange between Negroponte and Grameenphone founder Iqbal Quadir: "Communication Breakdown," *Good*, December 18, 2008.

3. Economists have found in Kenya, for example, that treating children for parasitic worm infections in places where intestinal worms are endemic can dramatically improve school attendance and by extension education outcomes. Ten years after the original study, treated individuals were earning as much as 25 percent more than their peers who weren't treated.

Another study compared a computer-assisted learning application with a program that assigned minimally trained teacher's assistants to work one-on-one or in small groups with low-performing students in India. The study found that the teacher's assistants consistently improved literacy and numeracy of the children they worked with at significantly lower cost than the computer programs. Other studies on computer-assisted education in other contexts have shown mixed, often negative, results. For more information, see Edward Miguel and Michael Kremer, "Worms: Identifying the Impacts on Education and Health in the Presence of Treatment Externalities," *Econometrica* 72, no. 1 (January 2004): 159–217; Edward Miguel, Michael Kremer, Sarah Baird, and Joan Hamory Hicks, "Worms at Work: Long-Run Impacts of Child Health Gains," http://www.poverty-actionlab.org/publication/worms-work-long-run-impacts-child-health-gains; and Abhijit Banerjee, Shawn Cole, Esther Duflo, and Leigh Linden, "Remedying Education: Evidence from Two Randomized Experiments in India," *Quarterly Journal of Economics* 122, no. 3 (2007): 1235–1264.

4. This story was recounted by Quadir in: "Communication Breakdown."

5. See study results from the 2006 Accenture survey of 580 executives conducted by the Economist Intelligence Unit. The executives came from more than a dozen different countries and were asked about their merger and acquisition activities, both in-country and cross-border. The data shows that 48 percent of respondents believe the merger achieved expected cost savings, and 52 percent of respondents believe the merger achieved revenue targets. Most of the mergers were in-country, not cross-border. The study also shows that only 10 percent of executives strongly believe that their firms are skilled at executing cross-border deals. See "Integrating Acquisitions," Economist Intelligence Unit, April 2006, http://graphics.eiu.com/upload/eb/Integrating_acquisitions.pdf.

6. "China's First Global Capitalist," *Bloomberg BusinessWeek*, December 11, 2006, http://www.businessweek.com/magazine/content/06_50/b4013062.htm.

7. Paul Lawrence, *Driven to Lead: Good, Bad, and Misguided Leadership* (San Francisco: Jossey-Bass, 2010).

8. For more information on GLOBE, see http://www.thunderbird.edu/sites/globe/.

9. For details of how Toyota adapted its approach when it began manufacturing in the United States while keeping its culture and leadership model intact, see Jeffrey Liker and Gary Convis, *The Toyota Way to Lean Leadership* (New York: McGraw Hill, 2012).

10. In addition to openness, the Big Five traits include conscientiousness, extraversion, agreeableness, and neuroticism. This psychological model evolved from an ongoing body of work in the psychology field that focused on defining, identifying, and zeroing in on traits or aspects that make up one's "personality." The Big Five was first proposed by U.S. Air Force researchers Ernest Tupes and Raymond Chrystal, and validated and refined by Warren Norman.

11. Janine Nahapiet and Sumantra Ghoshal, "Social Capital, Intellectual Capital, and the Organizational Advantage," *Academy of Management Review* 23, no. 2 (1998): 242–266, http://www.jstor.org/stable/259373.

12. Geert Hofstede, *Cultures and Organizations, Software of the Mind: Intercultural Cooperation and Its Importance for Survival* (New York: McGraw-Hill, 1996).

13. For more information about the GMI, and for sample questions, see http://www.thunderbird.edu/knowledge_network/ctrs_excellence/global_mindset_leadership_institute/global_mindset_inventory.htm.

14. Excerpted from a blog post written by Raju Narisetti, http://shekharkapur.com/blog/2008/05/guest-blog-by-raju-narisetti-coming-home/.

15. "Myth Busters at Opera Software Deliver Internet to All," Thunderbird Knowledge Network Blog, http://knowledgenetwork.thunderbird.edu/research/2008/11/07/myth-busters-at-opera-deliver-internet-to-all/.

16. Conor O'Clery, *The Billionaire Who Wasn't* (New York: Public Affairs, 2007).

17. Information in this section is derived from David E. Bowen and Andrew Inkpen, "Exploring the Role of 'Global Mindset' in Leading Change in International Contexts," *Journal of Applied Behavioral Science* 45, no. 2 (June 2009): 239–260.

18. Ibid.

19. Thunderbird's curriculum has evolved through the years to provide a concentrated dose of global intellectual capital through three complementary mechanisms. First, the curriculum combines the traditional business core of an MBA with a set of courses geared toward understanding the cultural, institutional, and business realities of different regions. Second, all business courses are covered from a global perspective that explicitly embeds cases illustrating the complexities inherent in managing businesses across borders. Third, students are given a number of field-learning opportunities, so they can experience different environments firsthand and develop a discipline of exploration, such as learning what questions to ask and where to look for answers.

20. Nahapiet and Ghoshal, "Social Capital, Intellectual Capital, and the Organizational Advantage."

21. http://inmaps.linkedinlabs.com/.

Chapter 3

1. Quote from interview with Annie Duflo, 2009 Innovations for Poverty Action annual report.

2. See, for instance, C. A. Hidalgo, B. Klinger, A-L. Barabasi, and R. Hausmann, "The Product Space and Its Consequences for Economic Growth," *Science* 317 (2007): 482–487.

3. M. F. Guillén, *The Limits of Convergence* (Princeton, NJ: Princeton University Press, 2001).

4. http://blogs.hbr.org/cs/2011/09/why_someone_from_apple_needs_t.html.

5. Loretta Chao, "IPhone Gets Lukewarm Response in China," *Wall Street Journal*, October 30, 2009.

6. J. Quelch and K. Herman, *McDonald's*, Harvard Business School Case 508-025 (Boston: Harvard Business School, 2008).

7. Kishore Dash, "McDonald's in India," Case Series (Glendale, AZ: Thunderbird, 2005).

8. Miguel Bustillo, "After Early Errors, Walmart Thinks Globally to Act Locally," *Wall Street Journal*, August 14, 2009.

9. Nathan Washburn and B. Tom Hunsaker, "Finding Great Ideas in Emerging Markets: Why Your Managers Need to Double as Idea Scouts," *Harvard Business Review*, September 2011.

10. William Kamkwamba and Bryan Mealer, *The Boy Who Harnessed the Wind: Creating Currents of Energy and Hope* (New York: William Morrow, 2009).

11. Quote from an interview with Shai Agassi, Asia-Pacific Economic Cooperation conference in San Francisco, September 2011; Brad Berman, "Better Place's Shai Agassi: To Succeed, Plug-In Cars Better Beat 3-Minute Gas Fill Up," *Plug-In Cars*, September 29, 2011.

Chapter 4

1. See Ángel Cabrera, "Economic Truths," *Financial Times*, October 9, 2009. A video recording of the speech is available at http://www.youtube.com/watch?v=TME1GxiPUEU.

2. M. S. de Luque, N. T. Washburn, D. A. Waldman, and R. J. House, "Unrequited Profit: How Stakeholder and Economic Values Relate

to Subordinates' Perceptions of Leadership and Firm Performance," *Administrative Science Quarterly* 53, no. 4 (2008): 626–654.

3. Newt Gingrich, speech to Senate and House Republican campaign committees, Washington, DC, June 8, 2009.

4. For more information on Chiquita in Colombia, see http://www .cbsnews.com/video/watch/?id=5228111n; and Carol Leonnig, "Ex-Chiquita Execs Won't Face Bribe Charges," *Washington Post*, September 12, 2007.

5. For more information on Nike's experiences in Pakistan, see David Montero, "Nike's Dilemma: Is Doing the Right Thing Wrong?" *Christian Science Monitor*, December 22, 2006; and Syed Fazl-e-Haider, "Nike Bounces Back in Pakistan," *Asia Times*, May 31, 2007.

6. Michael Moss, "The Burger That Shattered Her Life," *New York Times*, October 2, 2009.

7. The term "Bottom Billion" was coined by Oxford economist Paul Collier in his book of the same name. The bottom billion refers to the citizens of the world's poorest countries, which are stuck in low-growth, low-prospect cycles because of one or more "traps." The four traps Collier highlights in his book include: the conflict trap, the natural resource trap, the landlocked with bad neighbors trap, and the poor governance trap. The governance trap is most closely relevant to our discussion of citizenship and corruption, though the traps are in fact interconnected and mutually reinforcing. See Paul Collier, *The Bottom Billion: Why the Poorest Countries Are Failing and What Can Be Done About It* (New York: Oxford University Press, 2007). Transparency International creates an annual global perceptions index that rates countries based on the amount of corruption that takes place in its business and government environments. The most recent index is available at http://www .transparency.org/policy_research/surveys_indices/cpi/2010.

8. Transparency International, "Transparency in Reporting on Anti-Corruption—A Report of Corporate Practices," http://www.transparency .org/publications/publications/2009_06_19_final_trac_report.

9. Asjylyn Loder and David Evans, "Koch Brothers Flout Law Getting Richer with Secret Iran Sales," *Bloomberg BusinessWeek*, October 3, 2011.

10. See, for example, Nicholas Kristof, "Where Sweatshops Are a Dream," *New York Times*, January 14, 2009.

11. Ann Harrison and Jason Scorse, "Moving Up or Moving Out: Anti-Sweatshop Activists and Labor Market Outcomes," working paper no. w10492, National Bureau of Economic Research, 2004.

12. Details and statistics on Intel's activities in Costa Rica come from the following sources: Roy Nelson, "Intel's Site Selection Decision in Latin America," *Thunderbird International Business Review* 42, no. 2 (March–April

2000), http://besana111.com/ileana/cursos/2011/IN2003/pdf/IntelCR_ sem8.pdf; Michael Metzger, Esteban Brenes, and Robert Holme, "Building a High-Technology Workforce: Electronics and Information Technology in Costa Rica," INCEA Research Center, INCEA Business School, Alajeula, Costa Rica, 2008 (photocopied document); "The Impact of Intel in Costa Rica: Nine Years After the Decision to Invest," World Bank Group, May 2006, https://www.wbginvestmentclimate.org/uploads/The%20 Impact%20of%20Intel%20in%20Costa%20Rica.pdf.

13. For details on these programs, see http://www.mectizan.org and http://www.gsk.com/community/public_health_programmes.htm.

14. For a more complete discussion of Toyota's challenges during the economic downturn, see Jeffrey Liker and Timothy Ogden, *Toyota Under Fire* (New York: McGraw-Hill, 2011).

15. The proverb in Spanish is: *Dime con quién andas y te diré quién eres.*

16. For more details on the principles, see http://www.unprme.org/.

17. Ángel was chairman of the task force that authored the principles.

18. Mary Gentile, *Giving Voice to Values: How to Speak Your Mind When You Know What's Right* (New Haven, CT: Yale University Press, 2010).

19. Rakesh Khurana and Nitin Nohria, "It's Time to Make Management a True Profession," *Harvard Business Review*, October 2008.

20. Klaus Schwab, "Shaping a Post-Crisis World," *New York Times*, February 7, 2009.

21. For more information on the Oath Project, see http://www.theoath-project.org.

22. http://www.facebook.com/Artemis.Pakistan.

Conclusion

1. Benjamin Friedman, *The Moral Consequences of Economic Growth* (New York: Knopf, 2005).

2. "Widespread Unease About Economy and Globalization," World Public Opinion, February 7, 2008, available at http://www.worldpublic-opinion.org/pipa/articles/btglobalizationtradera/446.php?lb=btgl&pnt=446.

3. Brian Montopoli, "Poll: 43 Percent Agree with Views of 'Occupy Wall Street,'" *CBS News*, October 25, 2011, http://www.cbsnews.com/8301-503544_162-20125515-503544/poll-43-percent-agree-with-views-of-occupy-wall-street/.

4. For a review of the available literature on how management practice affects corporate outputs, see Chad Syverson, "What Determines Productivity?" *Journal of Economic Literature* 49, no. 2 (2011): 326–365.

Notes

5. Nicholas Bloom, Aprajit Mahajan, David McKenzie, and John Roberts, "Why Do Firms in Developing Countries Have Low Productivity?" *American Economic Review: Papers & Proceedings* 100, no. 2 (2010): 619–662.

6. Joris Lammer, Diederik Stapel, and Adam Galinsky, "Power Increases Hypocrisy: Moralizing in Reasoning, Immorality in Behavior," *Psychological Science* 21, no. 5 (May 2010) 737–744.

7. Jonah Lehrer, "The Power Trip," *Wall Street Journal*, August 14, 2010.

ACKNOWLEDGMENTS

We owe this book to Thunderbird. Our home institution is not only our employer but our main source of information, insight, and inspiration. We met many of the global leaders we highlight in this book at Thunderbird, and much of the academic work that underlies our model came from our Thunderbird colleagues.

The "Global Mindset" chapter draws directly from the work of the Global Mindset Institute, led by Mansour Javidan, as well as the GLOBE project, to which Mary Sully de Luque has made deep contributions. Our views on global entrepreneurship and strategic leadership can be traced to work by our colleagues Kishore Dash, Bob Hisrich, Andrew Inkpen, Michael Moffett, Kannan Ramaswamy, Andreas Schötter, and Nathan Washburn, among others. The insights on how to become global draw from our experiences with our degree and executive programs and have been influenced by Robert Widing, our former provost, and David Bowen, our current provost. We are also grateful to the students and alumni of Thunderbird—we feel privileged to have taught and learned from them.

The Lincoln Center for Ethics in Global Management, generously sponsored by Thunderbird trustee and friend David Lincoln and his wife Joan, supported Gregory Unruh since his arrival at Thunderbird and provided the help we needed to complete this work. Our colleague Chelsea Oyen kept us on track with our timeline, and Daryl James wrote some of the case studies we feature. Timothy Ogden and Laura Starita of Sona Partners provided invaluable editorial assistance and kept us on topic and on task as we wrote the book.

The World Economic Forum's Young Global Leaders, several of whom are featured in the book, inspired us to write the book and reaffirmed our conviction that global leaders not only can be made, but are badly needed to deal with the opportunities and challenges of today's global marketplace.

Thanks to you all for the insights and inspiration you have gifted us. We hope we've done justice to your ideas and life stories.

Finally, our wives, Beth Cabrera and Silvia García Gans, as well as our children, Alex and Emily Cabrera and Enrique and Jesse Unruh, not only put up with us as we worked on this book, but have been incredibly understanding and fun travel partners during each of our own journeys toward *being global*.

INDEX

Index

ABOUT THE AUTHORS

Ángel Cabrera is President of Thunderbird School of Global Management, which is widely recognized as the number-one school in the international business field, and President-elect of George Mason University. Before coming to Thunderbird, he was Dean and professor of IE Business School in Madrid. A native of Spain, Cabrera earned his PhD and MS in psychology from the Georgia Institute of Technology, which he attended as a Fulbright Scholar, and a BS and MS in engineering from Madrid Polytechnical University, Spain's premier engineering school. He has authored numerous papers for leading academic journals and conferences and is often quoted by international media on global business issues and education.

An outspoken advocate for business global social responsibility, Cabrera advises the United Nations Global Compact in academic affairs; in 2007, he chaired the international committee that authored the Principles for Responsible Management Education. The World Economic Forum recognized him as a Global Leader for Tomorrow in 2002 and a Young Global Leader in 2005. In 2008, he chaired the Global Agenda Council for Promoting Entrepreneurship. In 2004, *BusinessWeek* named him a "Star of Europe" and in 2011, the *Financial Times* listed him among the top twenty business school deans in the world. He is an Aspen Institute

H. Crown Fellow and founder of The Oath Project, a foundation that promotes managerial professionalism around the world.

Gregory Unruh is the Director of the Lincoln Center for Ethics in Global Management at the Thunderbird School of Global Management and a well-known sustainability expert. After nearly a decade in corporate environmental consulting, Unruh pursued a career of research and publication dedicated to identifying and spreading the sustainability innovations needed by business and the world. A frequent contributor to the *Harvard Business Review*, *Forbes*, and the *Huffington Post*, Unruh is also the author of *Earth, Inc.: Using Nature's Rules to Build Sustainable Profits*, a leading guide to sustainable business strategy. He is also an inspirational public speaker and has presented at prestigious events such as the World Economic Forum, the Clinton Global Initiative, and the United Nations Global Compact. He can be contacted through his website at www.gregoryunruh.com.